BLAME IT ON THE MUSIC

BY

ERIC THOMPSON JR

BLAME IT ON THE MUSIC

Published by Eternal Royalty Publishing Company

Copyright © 2015 by Eric Thompson Jr

All rights reserved. No part of this book may be reproduced or transmitted in any form or by any means, electronic or mechanical, including photocopying, recording, or by any information storage and retrieval system, without permission in writing from the publisher.

ISBN: 978-0-692-41674-7

Although every precaution has been taken to verify the accuracy of the information contained herein, the author and publisher assume no responsibility for any errors or omissions. No liability is assumed for damages that my result from the use of information contained within.

www.dirtiminds.com

Dedicated

To My Beloved Mother

Beverly Laniece Reynolds

First of all I want to say Mama we made it. I truly wish that you were here to share this moment with me. Even though you're no longer here with us physically your light continues to shine bright. Your death taught me that there was no obstacle too great to overcome, I Love You Forever! To all my lost loved ones, you all inspire me every single day.

Acknowledgements

Special thanks goes to my father Eric Thompson Sr. I'm proud to be your son, you've inspired me more than you could ever know. I could fill this book with names of people who have played a major role in the manifestation of my dreams. My sisters ShaMeka, RaeNesha, TyMaiya, and Aliyah you all share a special place in my heart. I credit you four with getting on my nerves so much that I had to put my headphones on to drown out the noise. A very special thanks goes out to Cryss Walker of Radio One and Chief Editor of Top Flight Magazine. I'm forever indebted to you for allowing me the opportunity to fulfill a dream by writing for your magazine. Thanks goes to my brother Donte (Red), you paved the way by releasing your first book. I have too many family members and close friends to name individually; I want each of you to know that you've impacted me in some way and my first book is a result of that impact. A special thanks to my boys Chris Dorsey and Pat Webb, you two were the only people who donated to my Go Fund Me Account. I appreciate you both for supporting and believing in my dream.

BLAME IT ON THE MUSIC

Introduction

One of the earliest memories I have of rap music occurred when I was in elementary school. There was a song by Bone Thugs N Harmony that had someone speaking right before the song came on. The person said, *"We're not against rap, were not against rappers, But we are against those thugs."* Those words replayed in my head my entire life. At an early age I learned that rap music was controversial, I always heard rappers speaking about politicians and vice versa; too often in America problems of society are blamed on rap lyrics. Musical artists are messengers, the music they make usually represents their life experiences. Critiquing their music is basically saying that what they've been through doesn't matter. Judgmental people will never be able to understand this perspective, they just want to find someone to blame for the problems of the world. I do understand that artists are viewed as role models and their words are taken literally by some listeners. Some negative music becomes the soundtrack to misguided children's lives, I don't like the lifestyle some of these entertainers portray. Obviously if we search hard enough we can find evil in anything. We've all been inadequately taught about the Illuminati and all the behind the scenes propaganda that represents the music industry. Negativity is embraced and celebrated throughout every form of entertainment in this country, but that doesn't mean that every rap song is bad. When I was a senior in high school I threw every CD I owned in the trash after hearing a church sermon about the truth behind Hip-Hop. (Thank You Mrs. Cargill for reminding me of this.)

BLAME IT ON THE MUSIC

This book is not really for readers; of course you have to know how to read to enjoy it. Honestly I wrote this for music lovers and the many people who represent the Hip-Hop culture. I want you to hear and feel the songs as you read along. Music made me want to inspire the youth, it made me be proud of being black. Music made me respect women and recognize that I am a KING, music made me follow my dreams. BLAME IT ON THE MUSIC Hip-Hop made me do this.

Now before you start reading the stories I want you to know that this isn't your ordinary book. My whole point of writing this was to share some of my favorite rap songs and also share my inner most thoughts. I intentionally left this book void of chapters, every page is a journey of its own. I hope to empower my readers to break the mold, life doesn't have to be so mundane. You can literally open this book to any page and get started. These songs are all a part of my growth and I can say that they all represent either something I've been through or witnessed throughout my life.

BLAME IT ON THE MUSIC

1

"He said I write what I see

Write to make it right don't like where I be

I'd like to make it like the sights on TV

Quite the great life so nice and easy."

Lupe Fiasco

BLAME IT ON THE MUSIC

Artist: Lupe Fiasco feat. Nikki Jean

Album: The Cool (2007)

Hip-Hop Saved My Life

The whole point of me writing this book was to show the positive influence music, especially Hip-Hop artists have had on my personal life. I also want to highlight how much more than music Hip-Hop really is, it's a culture of misfits making art with their voices. Too many people believe that voting is our voice, I completely disagree. Rap music is the voice for oppressed people, the entire culture of music can be considered our voices. Without it we probably would have never heard of Tupac or Biggie, Jay-Z didn't stand a chance surviving the street life for as long as he has topped the music charts. Nas wouldn't have been able to school us on our roots, Scarface would probably still be on the streets and E-40 would have never been able to introduce his lingo. There are many more artists that could have been mentioned, I listen to a variety of them and I could produce a hundred books on their impact on society. With that being said allow me to share how much I appreciate the contributions of Hip-Hop, I gained a level of confidence listening to rap music. Tupac Shakur has spoken to me more than any individual I've ever crossed paths with and I never met him, which showed me that there is power behind music. Even in his death Tupac's voice can't be silenced. I gained insight about my past and roots from Africa blasting tracks by Nas and Lauryn Hill. Kanye West showed me that voicing my opinion on social issues is my right as a human being. Lupe showed me that it's cool to come from the hood and still be

BLAME IT ON THE MUSIC

intelligent. Big Sean allowed me to see a skinny black kid from Detroit become a global sensation and remain humble. I have a friend in Europe, as I'm writing this book, living his dream of passionately seeking change through his music. Out Kast and TLC showed us all that it's cool to be different. The Fab Five sporting baggy shorts and long black socks is a part of the culture of Hip-Hop, as well as the image of braids and tattoos that Allen Iverson made look so damn cool. I would have never heard of Huey P. Newton if it wasn't for music. I can go on and on about the correlation between Hip-hop and the exposure it has provided me. Hip-hop music has got me through my rough days, it taught me that anything is possible. I share the same sentiment as Lupe Fiasco and Nikki Jean when I say, Hip-hop has saved my life.

BLAME IT ON THE MUSIC

2

"It's time for us as a people to start making some changes

Let's change the way we eat, let's change the way we live

And let's change the way we treat each other."

Tupac Shakur

BLAME IT ON THE MUSIC

Artist: Tupac Shakur

Album: Greatest Hits (1999)

Changes

In a very ironic way Changes was the first song that I wrote about, it impacted my thoughts as a youth. When I was a sophomore in High School I had a class project where I had to pick a song that spoke on social or political issues, I chose Changes by Tupac. When Pac rhymed it wasn't just viewed as entertainment, he spoke with command and passion directly from his heart. He brought up topics and issues that most people would've rather ignored. This song forced me to really take heed to the message Pac was relaying, I wasn't a person who paid attention to music lyrics back then. Changes was different, the thought provoking song penetrates the listeners soul. Tupac spoke about his thoughts of suicide, poverty, war, racism, and even police brutality. It's so intriguing to me because he gave the young black male's perspective on a lot of issues. It's very important to me that I acknowledge anyone who has a positive message to share with Black Men. Changes addresses the problems that are common in ghettos all over the world. After pointing out the fact that we are all victims of an inadequate system, Shakur offers advice on how we can combat these problems. Tupac spoke about his thoughts of hopelessness, but he also tried to strive towards making positive progress. Pac taught me who Huey P. Newton was, which later explained his revolutionary persona. He spoke about the future and mentioned that the world wasn't ready to have a Black president. There is no doubt in my mind that Tupac was on

BLAME IT ON THE MUSIC

the verge of challenging this country's political system and inadequacies. He struck fear into the hearts of many politicians who refused to listen to his words. He addressed genocide amongst blacks and he begged for unity as a solution. Despite the world portraying him as a villain and a menace, this song is an example of his love for humanity. Tupac was a real man that didn't back down from his opposition. By deliberately seeking change and progress Mr. Shakur set an example for all leaders to follow.

3

"On my block, it's like the world don't exist, we stay confined to this small little section we living in.

On my block, I wouldn't trade it for the world, cause I love these ghetto boys and girls. Born and raised, On my block."

Scarface

BLAME IT ON THE MUSIC

Artist: Scarface
Album: The Fix (2002)

On My Block

Hickory

I love the story-telling that Scarface is known for. On My Block is a story for everyone. Most of us have specific areas where we were raised. That area could have been a housing project, apartment building or a residential neighborhood. The block I spent most of my life on was Hickory. I take pride when I say I was raised on HICKORY. The people that lived there will feel the same way, I'm sure. I learned how to hoop on my block. Back then we didn't care about going to the NBA; the goal was to be the best player on Hickory. Big Tone was the king of the backboard shot. We had so many fun times on that block back in the day. Barbeques and cookouts were routine for us on my block. The people I grew up with weren't just neighbors, we were a big family. I witnessed a lot of tragedy on Hickory as well. I saw a dead body for the first time walking home from elementary school. The whole hood was hurt when Tiffany died in that car crash. I still remember the shock of hearing that Darnell passed away. I saw broad day shootouts, group fights, drug sales and drug use. My block was no different from any other street in the hood. None of the behavior I witnessed frightened me, we were all accustomed to it. With all the negative things I recalled, I can recollect the good times the most. When we sat in the house and the windows began to rattle and shake, everyone knew it was Robbie D blasting his sounds. If I received an early knock on my door, it was probably Milford, he never wanted nothing either. If I walked outside and seen somebody fighting, nine times out of ten it was Juice. Whenever I heard basketballs bouncing it was DeTae dribbling up the block. Fast talking and curse words meant that Niecy was yelling at Wanda, Danielle, or Juanita. I will never forget when Kelly set Calvin's clothes on fire imitating Angela Basset in Waiting To Exhale. When I heard a ton of laughter I could almost guarantee it was Kevin or Ram baking Deshawn. The two kids always getting in trouble were Alan and Kape. Meka had the best birthday party ever next door in Re Re's backyard. Ant was the person that everyone wanted to race. Gangsta and Moe kept the dice games going on the corner. The soul food was always served by Deborah. Anybody that wanted to play the latest video games went to the twin's (Aaron, Anton) house. Sherry and Shana were the ones to go to if you needed your hair done. The broke down cars always found their way to our house, Pops was the neighborhood mechanic. Cube was the grown kid on the block and Hamburger Steak (Dre) had the funniest nickname ever. When I drive down Hickory now it looks like a ghost town; there are few houses left and all of my friends have moved away. No matter what though, we will always have the stories: I will represent HICKORY forever.

15Mile/ The Village

I can't talk about my childhood experiences without mentioning the time spent in The Village. I was eleven years old when my mother decided it was time for us to move to Clinton Township, MI. I had never heard of the city before, all I knew was that 15 mile was far. We lived in the front, the first house going towards Harper. The first thing I remember about moving there was hearing how bad The Village was supposed to be. I was warned to never go to the back at night time. Since there was a full basketball court back there I didn't mind risking my safety, I grew up on 6 and 7 mile. My friends on Hickory thought we were moving to the real suburbs. Anybody familiar with the Clinton Twp. area knows that The Village is definitely the hood. I used to go pay our rent to Ms. Alice (R.I.P) in the little office building. This was before I knew anything about low income or section 8 housing. I looked at my mother like she was a fool when she handed me $2 and told me to go pay the rent. I met some of my closest friends while adventuring on 15mile. I attended a middle school and high school that was pretty diverse as far as attendance. Most of my free time was spent at The Village basketball court. This was a place for new people to make a name for their selves. Since almost everybody had a nickname, it was only right that I got mine as well. My nickname had little to do with my basketball abilities. My childhood friend and basketball adversary Tone started calling me Chia, because he thought my afro looked like a chia pet. All my boys spent many summer days and nights on The Village court, except for the days the skunks decided to take over. We used to be pissed when the lights went out or when Chamar and Duce were out torturing people. The court was where the girls came to show off their outfits and watch the boys hoop. The dope boys parked their cars in the lot showing off their rims and blasting their sounds. I saw fiends get served, beat up and dunked on trying to hoop. Although the Village wasn't perfect I'm proud to have called it my home. I miss running around the hood playing football, hooping and just being around friends and even though the rims are gone, we still have the memories.

4

"We put shit on layaway then come back
We claim other people kids on our income tax
We take that money, cop work then push packs to get paid
And we don't care what people say."

Kanye West

BLAME IT ON THE MUSIC

Artist: Kanye West
Album: College Dropout (2004)

We Don't Care

This song is like an anthem for most people who grew up in the ghetto, we're only exposed to so much in our neighborhoods. *"As a shorty I looked up to the dope man, only adult man I knew that wasn't broke man."* (Kanye West) In the hood dope boys are symbols, they represent power, style and "success". Obviously it's all temporary, but try telling that to the kids who never had anything. The drug dealers also represent freedom, if that's even possible. They don't have to punch a clock and slave for seven dollars an hour. Selling dope is a trap and we all know it but it's still being done. We all have dreams of having enough money and freedom to live comfortable lives, especially the people who have been born into impoverished lifestyles. The people we often see doing this are the dope boys, they have the cars, the women, nice homes and clothes. I believe in making an honest living because that's what I was exposed to in my household. I watched my father go to work for a minimum of eight hours a day and at least five days a week for the past twenty six years of my life. The problem is I have watched my family struggle during these years. Meanwhile the guy around the block sold something in a bag and got money all day long. He didn't have to struggle, he went on trips and spent quality time with his children on a regular basis. Do you get what I'm trying to say? The truth is that most people sell drugs out of a sense of hopelessness, then it becomes rewarding. When anyone gets rewarded for something that's easy, they try to continuously do it. The thought of getting caught is rarely a deterrent in most cases. Jail is a guarantee for any black person dealing any type of drugs. Personally I wouldn't resort to it, but I also don't want to slave for the next thirty years of my life. Finding out my niche and where I fit into society is a current journey that I've been on and whether it's right or wrong this is our song. Thank You Mr. West!

BONUS: I remember when this song first came out I sat on Deborah's porch on Hickory with Robbie D and Kevin, we all emulated Kanye rapping the lyrics. Me and Kevin later laughed about this because Robbie didn't know all the words. It didn't matter though because this song represented him. R.I.P. Big homie

BLAME IT ON THE MUSIC

5

"I'm slippin I'm fallin I can't get up
Aye yo I'm slippin I'm fallin I can't get up
Aye yo I'm slippin I'm fallin I gots to get up
Get me back on my feet so I can tear shit up."
DMX

BLAME IT ON THE MUSIC

Artist: DMX

Album: Flesh of My Flesh, Blood of My Blood (1998)

Slippin

Life is full of challenges and obstacles, it really is an everyday task to stay positive. Having so much stress surrounding you can cause you to slip into negativity and make bad choices. There are days when you can feel like you've slipped so far that you can't recover, it's as if your problems have finally defeated you. Along with the everyday struggles we face, there's poverty, violence, drugs, racism, etc. The older I get the more adversity seems to surface in my life. Where I'm from the circumstances we grew up in breeds warriors, people who can overcome almost any obstacle. It becomes a way of life, we're accustomed to surviving. On the other hand, there are also a large amount of people who (slip) encounter hard times and never recover. Both examples exist for us all to see. Every day I am guaranteed to see at least one homeless person asking for change and I also hear of, or learn about a person dying violently. Encountering these situations will most definitely show you what you're made of as a person; they can either make you or break you. The time I personally felt at my lowest was when my mother passed away, it was on my thirteenth birthday. As a young man I didn't know how to feel. I was depressed, stressed, frustrated and afraid. I thought my life was over. My heart felt like it was physically ripped out of my chest. The one person I just couldn't imagine living without was gone forever with no warning or no farewell. As I stand now, a twenty seven year old man, I'm still bothered by this tragedy. I spent most of my days searching for someone to blame, sometimes I even blamed myself. I always asked why and I still haven't received an answer. What I learned about myself during these passing years is how much strength I really possess. I endured this heartache almost all alone, sure I had family around me, but no one could relate to the pain I felt. I actually felt like giving up so many times over the years, thank God I made it through this. My life is a testimony that no matter how low a person falls, they can always get back up.

6

"All that I been givin
Is this thing that I've been livin
They got me in the system
Why they gotta do me like that
Tried to make it my way
But got sent on up the highway
Why, oh why
Why they gotta do me like that?"
Anthony Hamilton

BLAME IT ON THE MUSIC

Artist: Jadakiss feat. Anthony Hamilton
Album: Kiss of Death (2004)

Why?

The mysteries of life leaves room for plenty of questions, everyone has wondered something before. Why is a remarkable way of challenging the status quo. This world and society trains most people to be passive and accept its conditions. "Never challenge authority, don't question God and you better not say anything controversial about the government." When a person asks a simple question like why, it's as if they ignited a riot. Of course true rebels marvel over the opportunity to stir things up by asking the questions. I'm sure we all have so many inquiries, life itself can be a huge mystery at times. This song is the total opposite of being politically correct. I've learned that most people would rather keep all their inquires bottled up inside of their mind, afraid to challenge people's minds and search for answers. I understand why though, it's like society frowns upon the people who don't fall in line. As a little kid we've all been met with anger when we ask too many questions, which further creates fear and leaves us void of basic knowledge. There have been some questionable things happening in the world lately. As a young black man growing up in a highly impoverished area, I definitely have a ton of questions; questions that no one seems to care to answer or even converse about. I can accept when people admit to not having all the answers. I respect the honesty it takes to say, "I don't know". On the other hand, I can't stand people who call me wrong for having a curious mind. One of the problems with the world is there aren't enough people willing to challenge these corrupt systems that are in place. We know the wrongs being committed, not enough people

BLAME IT ON THE MUSIC

care; I often wonder, why? Jadakiss really put together a list of questionable things that were going on in the world at this time (2001-2004). I admire the man for allowing his art form to be thought provoking and also just be an overall good song. He wasn't afraid to ask the tough questions, even though people with the answers weren't willing to honestly respond. A lot of the questions presented in this song will never be answered, I wonder WHY?

7

"Don't go chasing waterfalls

Please stick to the rivers and the lakes that you're used to

I know that you're gonna have it your way or nothing at all, but I think you're moving too fast."

BLAME IT ON THE MUSIC

Artist: TLC

Album: CrazySexyCool (1994)

Waterfalls

TLC was one of the most influential groups in the music industry. They were ahead of their time and an inspiration to people all over the world. Waterfalls is a song that will always be relevant. We all live in a microwave society, when we want something we expect it right away with no exceptions. Most of us aren't willing to take our time with anything, we frequent fast-food restaurants, because it's the quicker option. Overall our immediate goals are centered on having instant gratification. Young kids have sex without fully understanding the impact it will have on their bodies and minds in the future. The youth try to be adults way too fast, not realizing the trials that awaits them. Most of us lack the discipline it takes to actually listen to our elders. We've all been at a point in our lives where we think that we know everything. On the contrary, there are people who don't have a positive role model showing them how to live; this makes the fast life so enticing. I used to wonder why so many young people wound up on the streets. It's not because of their lack of vision, they're just seeing the wrong pictures. They see the drug dealers and the strippers earning the quick cash and they decide they want in. I feel like children from the ghetto are vulnerable. Our families fail us, the school system fails us as well as most of the churches. All this leads us to the streets which chews us up and spits us out, all because we look for validation from outside sources instead of searching within. I'm not making excuses either, this is a harsh reality. It doesn't have to be this way though. My advice to the young people coming up is to slow down enough to find out what you really want out of life, learn to pace yourself and God will grant you the desires of your heart.

BLAME IT ON THE MUSIC

8

"A perfect smile is more appealing but it's funny how

My shit is crooked look at how far I done got without it

I keep the twisted grill just to show the kids it's real

We ain't picture perfect but we worth the picture still."

J-Cole

BLAME IT ON THE MUSIC

Artist: J-Cole
Album: Born Sinner (2013)

Crooked Smile

Poor people often sit around fantasizing about how different things will be when they finally get rich. Coming from poverty, I know this scenario all too well. We're all born with unique characteristics, but instead of viewing our differences as something positive we often call them flaws. Having this mindset will never allow us to see and embrace our uniqueness. Instead we waste our time trying to fit into the world's image of how everything should look. Obviously it's about having confidence in ourselves, a lot of people aren't taught self-confidence growing up. We end up searching for ways to fix our "imperfections". Most of the solutions we find are not natural and tend to cause us serious problems in the long run. I have seen so many women getting butt and breast implants which are unnatural enhancements. I can't deny the eye candy these changes provide for us men, but all it will ever be is a way to feed men's lustful desires. Black people who are born with large noses and lips are often viewed as deformed or flawed. We've all seen the celebrities getting plastic surgery to change things they were born with. This is what happens when we allow others to define what beauty is to us personally. The Hollywood standard is what most people follow, not recognizing it's all a facade. It takes a big level of confidence and humility to accept the things that God blessed you with physically, especially when you're finally stable financially. Braces are another thing that helps people fix their smiles. I won't act like there aren't people who need them, it's just another unrealistic way of searching for perfection, in my opinion. I feel like our lives become

BLAME IT ON THE MUSIC

perfect when we figure out how to truly embrace and be comfortable with ourselves.

9

"I wrote these words for everyone who struggles in their youth

Who won't accept deception, instead of what is truth

It seems we lose the game, before we start to play

Who made these rules, we're so confused

Easily led astray."

Lauryn Hill

BLAME IT ON THE MUSIC

Artist: Lauryn Hill

Album: The Miseducation of Lauryn Hill (1998)

Everything is Everything

This is a very powerful song, Lauryn Hill wrote this for the true rebels. This world is so strange in many ways. It's so hard being a member of the youth. There are a groups of young people who just live life routinely and rarely seek to stand out, there's another group of children who want to truly know how things work. I was an observant person as a child and I was usually met with aggression and anger from my peers and most adults. At the time I didn't know why, I was just being myself. I was the kid that talked back and questioned authority when something I was told didn't make sense to me. Now I was taught to respect my elders, but I refused to show it to anyone who didn't respect me as well. As we all know most adults feel like kids should do what they're told, no questions asked. I refused to feel uncomfortable to stroke people's egos, so as a child I carried the bad kid label. I'll admit I did a few things to warrant the title, but I was just searching; I sought my place in the world trying to figure out where I fit in. A lot of my peers' parents said bad things about me and some wouldn't allow me to come over their house. I used to wonder why they thought so little of me, it hurt my feelings a lot back then. I now recognize why they didn't want me around, they couldn't allow their kids to take my lead and become inquiring and defiant. After mostly negative responses, I toned down my ways as a child: I just wanted to fit in and be seen as a normal kid. As an adult I proudly say that I'm back to my old ways, challenging the status quo and standing up for what I believe in. I will seek knowledge and wisdom for the rest of

BLAME IT ON THE MUSIC

my days. If you go into things with good intentions, what is meant to be will be. Thank You Lauryn Hill for relaying this message to me!

10

"Some say the blacker the berry, the sweeter the juice
I say the darker the flesh then the deeper the roots
I give a holler to my sisters on welfare
Tupac cares, if don't nobody else care
And uhh, I know they like to beat ya down a lot
When you come around the block brothas clown a lot
But please don't cry, dry your eyes, never let up
Forgive but don't forget, girl keep your head up."

Tupac Shakur

BLAME IT ON THE MUSIC

Artist: Tupac Shakur
Album: Strictly 4 My N.I.G.G.A.Z (1993)

Keep Ya Head Up

Life is full of ups and downs, terrible things happen every second of every day. Have you ever been through something that was so difficult that you knew you couldn't get over it? Have you ever lost someone very close to you, a person you couldn't imagine living without? If you answered yes to either of these questions then Keep Ya Head Up is speaking to you. Sad feelings and hard times can cause people to lose hope. Setbacks in life can either make or break the average person. The good thing about it is that it is all up to us as individuals, we have a choice. I have seen so many bad days and tragic situations growing up in Detroit. I have allowed some of the things I've witnessed and experienced to destroy me mentally. Luckily for me the defeat didn't last forever. When you come up in a rough neighborhood you develop a level of resiliency; it's like all the hardships become normal to you, which can be good or bad. Most of us become so immune to the destruction, that instead of challenging it we accept it. Single mothers raising those children all alone, KEEP YOUR HEAD UP! Children living off ramen noodles and hotdogs, KEEP YOUR HEAD UP! To all the kids whose parents are alcohol and drug addicts, KEEP YOUR HEADS UP! The message that Tupac was trying to get across was no matter what the circumstances are, we must hold our heads up high. We have to refuse to be defeated. So when you are having a rough day, a troubling week, or a hard life; you must remember that it doesn't have to last forever. The way we choose to think and react to our obstacles will ultimately determine the outcome. I'm no

BLAME IT ON THE MUSIC

expert or anything, but I would advise you all to KEEP YOUR HEADS UP!

Bonus: I remember being a ten year old kid and an older guy from my neighborhood was moving, his last words to me were to keep my head up. For a long time, I wondered why he said this to me. I finally have an understanding of what he meant, it's crazy to me because maybe he seen some of himself as a young man in me. It is that simple command that still inspires me over sixteen years later. How did he know the many trials that lied ahead for me? How did this man know that there would be times in my life where I would not want to live? Did he know that I would silently cry every night without anyone to wipe my eyes? I'm not completely satisfied with my life at the moment, but no matter what I go through I will always keep my head up!

11

"There's few writers in my cypher,
So they made lighter, my type of dreams seem dumb
They said wise up, how many guys you see making it from here
The world don't like us, is that not clear, alright
But I'm different, I can't base what I'm gone be off of what everybody isn't
They don't listen, just whispering behind my back
No vision, lack of ambition
So wack."

Jay-Z

BLAME IT ON THE MUSIC

Artist: Jay-Z
Album: The Blueprint 3 (2009)

So Ambitious

"The motivation for me is them telling me what I could not be."(Jay-Z)

We all have encountered people who attempt to limit our abilities. The world is full of doubters, critics and nay sayers. It's as if their job is to destroy the optimism of the individuals who dream big. I know that most people's criticism only mirrors their own insecurities. I've spent a great portion of my life trying to tell myself that I'm great and that my life matters. The true struggle for me was because I didn't hear encouraging words from my family members. Also every time I had great news to share it was as if it only mattered to me, we all want our family to be proud of our accomplishments. For as long as I can remember I have been surrounded by limited thinkers, their mindsets can be persuasive when you're searching for direction. I've had an adult tell me to my face that I wouldn't be shit and as heartbreaking as that was back then, I vowed to prove that person wrong. I realized that I couldn't let people be right, so I had to accomplish all of my goals. I believe all humans take mental notes of the doubts that were placed upon them. I made a list of the things that people said I wouldn't be able to do and with every success I cross it off. The ironic part about the criticism and disbelief is that it often comes from people who are close to us. I know parents who tell their kids that they're failures, teachers who call students dumb and coaches who say that their players aren't really talented. In life there's also times where you're shown how much people don't believe in you. Jobs not calling you back when you're more

BLAME IT ON THE MUSIC

than qualified, getting cut from the sports team and getting denied college admissions are a few that come to mind. If we allow them, the "failures" can crush our self-esteem. It's ironic how much an individual's self-esteem has little to do with their personal beliefs sometimes. There comes a time in every great person's life where they turn the doubts into ambition to propel them forward in life. We all have to learn how to say fuck the haters, don't allow anyone to limit your vision for yourself. The more we ignore the doubters the more room we allow ourselves to make an impact, all we have to do is believe. I've learned throughout my life that I don't need haters as my motivation. It shouldn't be about proving anyone wrong, becoming a personal success will do all the talking.

12

"I woke up this morning and figured I'd call you
In case I'm not here tomorrow
I'm hoping that I can borrow a piece of mind
I'm behind on what's really important
My mind is really distorted
I find nothing but trouble in my life
I'm fortunate you believe in a dream
This orphanage we call a ghetto is quite a routine."

Kendrick Lamar

BLAME IT ON THE MUSIC

Artist: Kendrick Lamar

Album: Good Kid: M.A.A.D City (2012)

Sing About Me

Growing up in the hood is rough, it's so depressing when you observe what's truly going on. People die every day over pointless things, normal citizens become addicts and not just to drugs. There are children who are forced to make grown up decisions way too early, stripped of their innocence with no say so. I've seen so many people disregard their morals just to get by. There's an unconscious level of hopelessness in the minds of most ghetto inhabitants. I feel as though it's the only way to keep yourself from going insane due to the surroundings. Sing About Me is a jewel in my eyes, it looks into the minds of young teens; teens that know deep down inside that they'll never see better days. They make decisions solely based on the present moment, there is no "future", it doesn't exist to them. I'm not saying that all ghetto children feel this way, I can only speak from my own experiences. The song is actually the teen's way of leaving their mark on the world. Kendrick's childhood friend asks him to promise that when he makes it as a rapper that he will sing about him after he's dead and gone. Imagine the feelings one must experience to know that there is no hope for them. So they place their legacy into the hands of someone who they know will make something of themselves. Gun violence plagues most urban "communities". Most young men accept their fate and fully immerse into terrible activities. The other teen Kendrick mentions in this song is a young lady who sells her body for money. She totally disregards the life threatening consequences of her actions, does this sound familiar to you? Where I'm from this is a normal day for most young ladies.

BLAME IT ON THE MUSIC

Hearing this song makes me emotional, it's as if I wrote the words myself. I'm the kid from the hood trying not to forget about anybody, I feel an obligation to become somebody great. Not only for me, but for all the kids/people who passed away before they could fulfill their dreams. I often wonder why I have these feelings but I don't shy away from them. It strengthens me to carry all the weight, sometimes I wonder if I'm strong enough to complete the tasks. I will continue to strive forward hoping one day I'll become an inspiration for someone to speak well about before I'm dead and gone.

13

"I shed tears and they won't come back
I said the word and they won't run back
My slot machine was broken this time
Isn't no tokens, I can't redeem to preserve the focus of mine
So many died and I'm scared it's just a matter of time
For I'm lifted myself, six people I know
Ain't been in church in a while, I heard I reap what I sow."

Big Krit

BLAME IT ON THE MUSIC

Artist: Big Krit

Album: King Remembered In Time (2013)

Life is a Gamble

We all know that in life we win some battles and we lose some. We go through things that we feel are unfair as well. I've never been a big believer in luck, so I rarely gamble. Then again that's only when it pertains to money, everyday life can actually be a bunch of crap games. We make choices without much thought that can have major impacts on our futures. Men and women engage in sexual activities with no protection, sometimes with complete strangers. Others pick fights with people, not knowing what the next person is capable of. Where I'm from the act of walking out your front door at the "wrong" time can be viewed as a calculated risk. This song has never been more real to me than this present time in my life. In May of 2013 I lost a childhood friend to gun violence. This guy was really a brother to me and I'm still in shock and disbelief that he's no longer alive physically. Obviously people die every day, it's actually a social norm to hear about or see someone grieving over a lost loved one. Willie (Stanky) was different, I say his name knowing that it can be substituted with so many others. He was good heart-ed young man with his whole life ahead of him. He was a family man with two young children who now have to suffer. The story is way too familiar, gone too soon is usually the chant. Well I guess God has the final say in that. It hurts because good people should be spared certain hassles, but my brother actually lost the battle. This situation makes me question, how will I go? It makes me consider what fate awaits me. We all have to face reality that one day will be our last, so we have to make the most of this life that we've been blessed with.

BLAME IT ON THE MUSIC

Bonus: For My Brother Stank (Willie Clark Jr)
I never actually thought I was invisible, I will admit I've felt invincible. For some reason I felt like nice guys actually got to live free of certain drama. I thought we were free from having to worry about bad things. Who would want to harm me? I show so much love to everyone. Reality is a true shock to me. I've watched a lot of people go through bad things. I lost people I loved to violent deaths, losing Stanky was one of the worst things I have been through. He was more than a friend he was my brother, it hurts so bad having to accept that he's gone. Add to that the fact that he was murdered, shot in the chest by someone he knew. Stanky was truly a loving, caring individual: he never really bothered anybody, he didn't deserve to go the way he did. He didn't deserve to die at all. We are really living in some hard times, innocent people dying every day. I feel as though my life has meaning, I also feel like Willie's life had meaning. Twenty four years young, he didn't even get to live out all of his dreams. I will carry Stanky in my heart every single day that I'm alive. Although the circumstances are fucked up, you inspire me brother. I promise to be great in your memory, see you when I get there!!

BLAME IT ON THE MUSIC

14

"We used to fuss when the landlord dissed us
No heat, wonder why Christmas missed us
Birthdays was the worst days
Now we sip champagne when we thirsty
Uh, damn right I like the life I live
Cause I went from negative to positive."
Biggie Smalls

BLAME IT ON THE MUSIC

Artist: Biggie Smalls
Album: Ready to Die (1994)

Juicy

I'm pretty sure that we all anticipate the days when our hard times will be over forever, even though life can't be perfect nobody wants to struggle their entire lives. Juicy by Biggie is a track that speaks about going from rags to riches, the day when you can finally silence the people who doubted you. Juicy also is a song to inspire the listeners to live the life they have only dreamed about. It's so exciting and rewarding when one can reflect back on life, especially if you have ascended from the bottom of the totem pole. For me personally it would mean so much to be able to provide a better life for not only myself but for my loved ones as well. I grew up in a household where we went without utilities often. Imagine having to take a cold shower in the winter time, or not having lights when you have to do homework. We had to walk around with flashlights and candles just to find something to wear. I used to be so embarrassed carrying buckets of water down the street, just to flush our toilet at home. I won't sit here and act like my entire childhood was this rough, but it wasn't all good days either. The tough living conditions really humbled me; I tried not to judge people, because I never knew what others went through secretly. Through all of my obstacles I developed a level of ambition. I refuse to allow my children (when I have some) to endure the hardships I faced as a youth. I strive to live free from the many worries that I was plagued with. I don't say this to critique my parents either, they worked really hard to provide for me and my siblings. After saying all of this, I still wouldn't change much of what I've been through if I had the opportunity. All of my experiences have molded me into

BLAME IT ON THE MUSIC

the great man that I am today. Just as this song has provided me with hope for a better future, I hope my words can do that for you. If you put your mind to it, you can turn your negative past into a very rewarding future.

15

"I don't wanna be another nigga,
Tell the government
I don't wanna be another nigga
Tell them white folk
I don't wanna be another nigga
Tell them black folk
I don't wanna be another nigga
Tell the world
I don't wanna be another nigga."
Big Krit

BLAME IT ON THE MUSIC

Artist: Big Krit
Album: Return of 4eva (2011)

Another Naive Individual Glorifying Greed and Encouraging Racism

I'm a very observant person and the people I have been watching my entire life have been living below their potential. As harsh as this might sound the people I've been around my entire life have disappointed me. I don't want it to seem like I think that I'm better than anybody, I just feel that we are all better than the way we live. I've striven to be different for as long as I can remember. I could never get used to being a vulnerable, government depending lazy person. Selling drugs wasn't something I saw myself doing and sleeping with a bunch of women never seemed like a major accomplishment to me. Violence and fighting all the time has always been something that I despised. Those were a few of the many things black children are exposed to way too early in their lives. It seems as if it's all we saw where I was raised. Our views of the world are often so limited, only representing the places that we grew up. As unfair as this is this was my reality, but all of my life I've worked hard to distance myself from the ghetto behavior. The problem I encountered was that I can't distance myself too far, it's a part of who I am today. The hard times and tough experiences mad me a resilient individual. I used to despise the negative behavior of my family, friends and peers. I was often very judgmental as well, but I didn't mean any harm. A part of me was just looking for guidance from the people I was familiar with. I could also see the enormous potential that my people possessed, so many lives have been wasted on these infested Detroit streets. It sickened me to witness all of these great people wasting their God given abilities. The older I get the more I realize how easy it is to get trapped, this uncomfortable lifestyle becomes too familiar and positive change is often scolded. We've all been conditioned to just go with the flow, no matter how right or wrong it may be. I can't just sit back and allow my life to pass me by. We all have higher levels that we can reach in every area of our lives, let's all ascend to the mountain top.

Bonus: The word Nigga, Nigger however it's used has always been controversial. It has very racist history and that isn't to be taken lightly. Just like every negative thing Blacks in America have been faced with, we've reversed this negative term into a word of endearment. I never understood why my elders got so angry as me and my friends used the word so freely, we meant no harm. I finally get it, words are so powerful. Imagine if Black men and women addressed each other as Kings and Queens, our behavior would have to mirror our greetings.

16

"Same old shit, just a different day
Out here tryna get it, each and every way
Momma need a house
Baby need some shoes
Times are getting hard
Guess what I'm a do?"
Ace Hood

BLAME IT ON THE MUSIC

Artist: Ace Hood
Album: The Statement (2010)

Hustle Hard

Quite often the word hustle gets lost in translation, it can mean so many different things. Sometimes negativity is an association of hustle, but most of the time it's actually a positive trait to possess. In sports, basketball in particular, hustling is a great action. It's the ability to be tenacious, strong willed and tough mentally. Players who carry these traits are an integral part of a winning team's success, the same is true about individuals who carry these characteristics in life. Each passing day comes with its own plots, themes and obstacles. We never know what type of situation might occur in our daily lives. All we can do is be willing and ready to overcome anything we're faced with. Ace Hood created a great song with Hustle Hard. Where I'm from a hustler can have many different titles and occupations. So if you're a rapper, stripper, college student, school janitor, teacher, mechanic, yes I'm talking to you; I don't care if you sell shoes, work at MC Donald's, flip houses, or work at Chrysler. We can all hustle harder to get where we truly want to be in our lives, it doesn't necessarily have to mean having more money or living in a better neighborhood. We can start exactly where we're at this very moment, all it takes is a willingness to get better. Being alive warrants room for improvement. A hustler can't be lazy at all, it takes commitment to manifest success. No matter how bad things seem, we all have choices. The quality of our lives evolve around the choices we make, so no matter what our motivation is we all must become relentless. Make up your

BLAME IT ON THE MUSIC

mind and refuse to be denied, whatever it is you want just hustle harder until it's yours.

17

"Stuntin like my daddy, I be stuntin like my daddy

I'm the young stunna, stuntin like my daddy

Stuntin like my daddy, I be stuntin like my daddy."

Lil Wayne

BLAME IT ON THE MUSIC

Artist: Lil Wayne

Album: Like Father, Like Son

Stuntin Like My Daddy

Every day we hear of someone paying homage to females and their mothers. As a black man I can say that our fathers are treated like the black sheep. Most of us are used to the story of dead beats and absent men. There aren't enough people out here praising the fathers who embrace the responsibilities of raising their children. I'll admit I haven't always been close to my father, but he has always been in my life. Up until I was an adult I didn't know if my dad actually liked me or not. The men I grew up around were all prideful, they didn't show much emotions or feelings, except for anger. I spent most of my childhood years attempting to be different from my father, I always heard people comparing my ways with his and it really annoyed me. I wanted to be my own person and it seemed as if I was living in his shadows. Now that we are actually close, I see that being like him isn't bad at all. I was very critical of my father because I didn't really know him; I listened to all the bad things that others said about him also. My father has sacrificed so much for me and my siblings. He took on a superman like role when my mother passed away. A lot of times he had no idea what to do but he always found a way. I want to let my pops know that I appreciate him and that his hard work and discipline has made me the man I am today, for that I am forever grateful! I feel ashamed because I grew up resenting my dad; I now know that he has always been a man of strength, character and charisma. I am the upgraded version of my father and I say that humbly, without his contributions in my life I would be lost. I am a midget standing on the shoulders of a giant and I can see much further as a result of my father's impact. I am delighted to show the world that there are Black men who deserve praise and honor.

Bonus: I appreciate the men who have been there to give me advice and insight on life. Gleo Wade was one of those men, he convinced me to run track when I was a high school freshman and he has taught me a lot about being a man. Maurice Clark, Kevin Thompson, Eric Rogers, Robert Townsend, John Reynolds Jr, Daryl Sanders, Keith Bond and Shawn Reynolds are all great men that I can say have encouraged me to be better. I appreciate each of you tremendously.

18

*"Here's a message to the newborns, waitin to breathe
If you believe then you can achieve
Just look at me
Against all odds, though life is hard we carry on
Livin in the projects, broke with no lights on
To all the seeds that follow me
protect your essence
Born with less, but you still precious
Just smile for me now."*

Tupac Shakur

BLAME IT ON THE MUSIC

Artist: Scarface and Tupac

Album: The Untouchable (1997)

Smile

I've heard that it takes more muscles to frown than it does to smile. Life gives us all so many reasons to be sad. There's destruction of this planet happening at a rapid pace, disease, famine and violence all give us viable things to frown upon. There's nothing funny about living in poverty. I'm not saying that impoverished people have no fun, it's just hard to do. I rarely ever smiled when I was a youth. When I was in high school, a teacher asked me why I never smiled. Being a music fan, I hit her with a 50 Cent line, *"I don't smile a lot cuz ain't nothin pretty."* She got mad at me, truth is I just wasn't happy. I wasn't able to clearly articulate my thoughts at the time. I had a lot of pain in my heart, so I felt few things were worthy of my smile. I felt all alone so I internalized most of my feelings. As an adult I can see the same in the eyes of some kids I come across, it's a painful sight for me. One thing that made me happy was playing basketball, it's still my favorite hobby. The sport allowed me the opportunity to release some of my stress and aggression in a positive way. Without basketball I don't know which direction my life would have went in. Despite the pain from our pasts, we have plenty of reasons to smile. The fact that air is still in our lungs is cause for celebration, we all know that the next breath isn't promised. It's up to us as individuals to stay positive throughout all the things we go through. I'm

BLAME IT ON THE MUSIC

not saying that there aren't moments where frowns and tears aren't required, it's just essential to our well-being that we learn to have joy as much as we can. Smiling is contagious, so we should all spread it as much as possible. If you feel like life offers you seldom reasons to have cheer, it is your duty to create it. We weren't created to spread hate and negativity, we're all blessed beyond comprehension and that's a great reason to smile.

19

*"A angel gave me love
I'm thankful, to ever know a woman so real
I pray when I marry my wife will have one of your skills
But mom you could never be replaced
I'd give my life up
Just to see you one more day."*

Nas

BLAME IT ON THE MUSIC

Artist: Nas

Album: God's Son (2002)

Dance

Dancing is something that is associated with music, you can't have one without the other. It's a form of expression with so many different styles. This song was made by Nas in memory of his late mother, he was reminiscing on all the times they shared. Nas said that he wished to have one more dance with his mother. Anybody who's ever lost a loved one can understand this song. When a person passes away, it's almost always devastating. It doesn't matter if the death was expected or a sudden tragedy, it's always tough to deal with. The reason is because there's a feeling of unfinished business, we all want to be around our loved ones forever. My mother passed away when I was thirteen years old, so I can definitely relate to this track. Her death was and still is the toughest thing that I've been through in my entire life. My mother and I never got the opportunity to dance with one another. I wish I could experience that moment, I long to talk to her now that I'm a man. I often wonder how our relationship would be now, would I had turned out any different if she was still here with me? Then there's the guilt I felt when she passed away, as a teen I didn't know how to deal with these emotions. Knowing a loved one is gone forever is extremely painful, I would have never imagined having to bury my mother. I never knew how much a boy needed his mother's love. Back then I didn't feel like my mother loved me, she always showed tough love, but as a kid I honestly thought it was hate. A fathers' job is to make their boys a man and mothers are there to nurture their children. It

BLAME IT ON THE MUSIC

angered me because I felt like I didn't get the proper nourishment as I grew up. When my mom passed away, I felt guilt and shame for being mad at her; I blamed myself for her death. I realized later on that it wasn't my fault, but I really miss her. I long to repair the rough relationship we had, I know others can feel my pain. I regularly ask her questions, I wish she would answer me. I hope that she's proud of me and I wish I could grab her hand and dance.

20

"I finally understand
for a woman it ain't easy tryin to raise a man
You always was committed
A poor single mother on welfare, tell me how
ya did it
There's no way I can pay you back
But the plan is to show you that I understand
You are appreciated."

Tupac Shakur

BLAME IT ON THE MUSIC

Artist: Tupac

Album: Me Against The World (1995)

Dear Mama

A very popular trend in music, especially in Hip-hop music, is paying homage to one's mother. We often show much appreciation for everything our mothers have done for us. I can't speak for other races, but in the black households our mothers are like God. They are the epitome of strength, they're beautiful, courageous and gentle. They play many roles as well: they're our doctors, teachers, cooks and chauffeurs. We argue with them and cry to them all the time. Our mothers get the blame for our bad behavior and credit for our good deeds. These beautiful women are there when we scrape our knees, when we experience our first heartbreak and when we say I do. Far too often women don't receive the proper respect for raising their children, especially black women. The commitment and strength it takes for women to be the head of households is unrivaled. Dear Mama is a song for every woman on this planet that has had a positive impact on someone's life. As previously stated in this book, I lost my mom at thirteen years old. I wasn't able to show her the proper appreciation while she was alive and well. She taught me so much about life in such a short period of time. Since her passing I've had many women become a motherly figure to me. That's a blessing that I gained, having the opportunity to have more than one mom. My aunt Sherry Reynolds has been there with me and my sisters every step of the way. Even though she has ten children of her own, she has always looked out for us: this is my way of saying I appreciate her so much. Also Andrea Harris, DarKesha Reynolds, Deborah Beamon, Denise Davis and Kimberly Thompson, I thank God for placing you beautiful ladies in my life. I hope that you all know that I'm proud of each of you and I hope you feel the same. Dear Mamas you are appreciated! To my angel Beverly Reynolds, I hope that you're smiling down on me and the girls. To my readers, if you have your moms or motherly figures in your life, celebrate and cherish them while you still have the chance.

21

"It's late in the day and I ain't been on the court yet
Hustle to the mall to get me a short set
Yeah I got on sneaks but I need a new pair
Cause basketball courts in the summer got girls there
The temperature's about 88
Hop in the water plug just for old times sake
Break to ya crib change your clothes once more
Cause you're invited to a barbeque that's starting at 4
Sitting with your friends cause y'all reminisce
About the days growing up and the first person you kiss."

Fresh Prince

BLAME IT ON THE MUSIC

Artists: DJ Jazzy Jeff and The Fresh Prince

Album: Homebase (1991)

Summertime

If you know anything about Michigan winters then you would understand why we all appreciate the summer time so much. The warm weather and shining sun is a constant reminder that, although it's sometimes tedious, life is beautiful and precious. Summer is a season that is highly anticipated, it's a time to make new memories and reminisce about the past. This song by Will Smith will make you do a lot of reflecting, younger people probably don't even know that Mr. Smith was a rapper first. This song came out in 1991, I was just three years old at the time. Despite its old school origins, Summertime will always be relevant. It's a part of the summer season, just like family reunions, barbeques and water balloon fights. There are so many things associated with the summer. You're guaranteed to see shiny rims, ladies in bikinis and street basketball as soon as the weather breaks fifty degrees. The sunshine can brighten your spirits, no matter what mood you're in. New shoes and clothes are a must have as soon as it gets hot; car washes get business all day long, because everyone wants their rides to look good. There are more sightings of drop tops and acrobatic motorcyclists. Carpooling to local parks and beaches is also a common cure to combat the high temperatures. There are a few negatives about the summer season as well. Most people can't stand the sight of bumble bees and mosquitoes, they represent a few creatures we all wish were extinct. Personally I despise rain in the summer, because it ruins the outside plans and activities. The summer season signifies the end of long school years. Here in Detroit we look forward to attending Summer Jams and frequenting Belle Isle and The River Walk. There are festivals, car shows and plenty of activities to occupy our time, all we need is a little sunshine.

BLAME IT ON THE MUSIC

22

*"Look, I'm talking Reggie Bush, matter of fact ask Cameron Newton
Matter of fact go ask they schools how many jerseys they was moving
Thank you for they tuition, thank you for room and board
Most of the niggas got no pot to piss during fall
Niggas sticking and moving, AJ flipping computers
Brandon Davis had relations, what if Jimmer was screwing?
They hate on Calipari, but I never seen the problem
They get one season and poppin shit, at least he's being honest."*

Wale

BLAME IT ON THE MUSIC

Artist: Wale

Album: The Eleven One Eleven Theory (2011)

Varsity Blues

Sports are a huge part of the culture in the world and they represent Hip-Hop. Sports bring people together who live different lifestyles and have major differences culturally. When you abide by the rules of particular sports, you're allowed to compete at dangerous levels. Have a good game and you can become a world-wide sensation. For all the positives that sports can provide, there is a dark side as well. Too often the people who suffer from this dark side are either seen as villains/rebels or they're completely forgotten. Athletes are often taken advantage of and used until they have nothing left to offer. Varsity blues by Wale vividly paints a picture, a picture on how unfair it is for top flight athletes. It is no coincidence that college athletes can't do anything to earn big money while they're receiving a scholarship to play. On the other hand, the schools earn unlimited amounts of money off the participation of these young amateurs. In the past few years there have been plenty of cases where the student athletes go out and earn money. In almost every instance they violate the rules, rules that are set up for the schools to make fortunes off the hard work of the student athletes. It's a violation to sell your possessions to earn money as a college player, even if you're poor. You can't give autographs for money, you can barely get money from your relatives without the ncaa taking a peek. It's truly like a slave plantation, where the master (universities) make billions off the blood, sweat and tears of the slaves (student

BLAME IT ON THE MUSIC

athletes). As harsh as this sounds, it's the truth. Not all of these players make it to the professional ranks and they're usually left bruised and broke (n). Also, they are never compensated for their efforts. I'm from a place where almost every young boy dreams of playing pro sports. Coming up I watched my peers get up every day in the summer to attend football practices. Often sports are seen as a way out of the poverty and violence we face on a daily basis. So the focus for the young athletes becomes to make it big. Anybody that displays the potential to go pro are viewed as a meal ticket, by family, friends, coaches etc. Many people line up waiting to see what they can leech off the naive stars, schools pitch why the kid should choose their university to continue their sports journey. Just as quick as they offer scholarships, they rescind them as well. If an athlete sustains an injury the interest diminishes. If the players have an inch of controversy they can lose their spot, it's a dangerous game that these young people are competing in and it's obvious who's losing.

Bonus: For every (Maurice Clarett) story of redemption, there are a million stories of these young men and women abandoned and left to fend for themselves. There's a large void in the lives of most young athletes, sports help fill that in some instances, but it goes south when the sports get taken away from them. The players get cheered and adored at their strongest and they're critiqued, mocked and forgotten at their weakest moments.

23

"This for every baller that fell short of hoop dreams

Everybody always saying don't forget about me when you make it

What if I don't?"

Money Cren

BLAME IT ON THE MUSIC

Artist: Money Cren

Album: Ball Playin Music (2013)

Untold Hoop Story

I didn't know who Money Cren was until I started following him on Instagram. I became immediately impressed with his unique perspective and point of view. This guy was a High School Phenom on the basketball court he also played Division 1 and overseas. This song really strikes a chord with me, I grew up with dreams of making it to the NBA. I know what it's like to have no thought out back-up plan. So many young black guys from the hood have the same aspirations. We usually view spots as our way out of the vicious lifestyle the ghettos present us with. It's like playing the lottery because going pro is not guaranteed for anyone. It's so many young guys who dream of being on the big screen, getting paid millions to hoop. The problem is that there's no way that everyone can make it. Aside from normal everyday obstacles that athletes have to deal with, there can also be injuries that will make them fall short of the professional ranks. Too many ball players depend solely on their physical abilities, instead of absorbing all that they can from the game mentally. The blame can be placed on the people that the athletes have around them, but ultimately they have to live with the consequences. I've watched people leech off of the stardom that young star athletes get, but disappear when that kid/player gets in trouble. I've seen guys go from can't miss prospects to drug dealers and prison inmates. There are so many individuals who were on top athletically and just didn't make it. This song is for the lost,

BLAME IT ON THE MUSIC

forgotten hoop stars; whether you were a street baller, a college bench rider or a pro.

24

"Go grab a mike or a ball son
How fucking backwards is that
Do you know the odds to make it in rap
And the chance to make it in hoop is even slimmer than that
You can't do one of the two, your only options to shoot
When the niggas you look up to on the block is not in a suit."

Jon Connor

BLAME IT ON THE MUSIC

Artist: Jon Connor

Album: Unknown

Don't Wanna Be

When I was younger I didn't really have any role models, I always saw flaws in everyone. I didn't understand that nobody was perfect, I realize this now that I'm an adult. The people I often emulated as a child were basketball players, rappers and entertainers. They were the people who looked similar to me and they had made something of their selves. To my knowledge they lived lives of luxury and abundance. Becoming an NBA player was my one and only goal back then, I knew that was my chance to rescue myself and my family. Now days I see the needs of these young children, they need a few ordinary people worth looking up to. The youth need someone to instill in them the power of being unique and different. I recognize these needs so much because I had the same ones earlier in my life. I feel sorry for these young women who watch TV searching for identity. The spotlight is not being placed on the women worthy of a following. All the shows are geared towards drama filled women and women who are okay sleeping with guys that are in relationships. The young men have a few more options, but it's not much; most of the guys are deemed useless if they can't entertain others. The things that are normal to urban kids are gruesome. We accept the fact that people sell drugs for a living, like there's no other options. Young girls aspire to be strippers in an attempt to find self-worth. Something must be done to challenge and change this behavior. This song by Jon Connor is him speaking on the subject of being different and challenging what's considered normal. He doesn't consider himself a rapper or entertainer, he knows that he is in a position to impact the lives of people in a positive way. Connor unselfishly uses his platform to shed light on subjects that need to be addressed in the hood. He has become an inspiration for others, by merely following his dreams and becoming the best person he can be. I now see how perfect my life has been shaping out, I am becoming the role model that I've searched for. I view myself as a normal guy with the capabilities to change the world. We all possess these abilities, anything we want to have is obtainable if we're willing to focus. Whatever you want out of life can be yours, all you have to do is put in the work necessary to get it. There's nothing greater than being the person that God created us to be.

25

"Remember that Christmas we had a wish list
We couldn't afford nothin but we still get shit ironically
Those were the times I felt the richest
All those times that we spent by the pool girl
Was too broke to even take you to the zoo girl
Maybe it's because I had you girl."

Big Sean

BLAME IT ON THE MUSIC

Artist: Big Sean

Album: Hall of Fame (2013)

Ashley

This song is something that a lot of people should be able to relate to. Does anyone remember being in "love" in grade school, how about your first kiss? Can you recall the times when you got butterflies in your stomach when you saw your special friend? Whether that person was just a crush or actually your companion, we should all remember our first relationships. It seems so long ago, but back then most of us only worried about what we would wear to school. I miss not having to go to work, the days when all I had to do was ask my parents for money to purchase Valentines and Christmas gifts. I miss the late weekend nights spent talking on the phone. In this song Big Sean speaks about his High School sweetheart Ashley, obviously the name can be substituted, but the message is all the same. Those younger relationships were the best, the ones that seemed as if they would last forever. We were all once naive enough to believe we would grow old with our teenage loves. Of course there are plenty of instances where young people stay the course and spend a lifetime of happiness with one another, things don't work out this way for the majority of us. Even if two people grow apart, they will always share the earlier memories. Those memories can last a lifetime. It doesn't matter how bad the relationships ended, or who was at fault. It doesn't matter if the person was the one that got away, or an example of what you don't want in a partner. We can all look back and laugh at how head over hills we once were. Those priceless moments are something we shouldn't want to trade for anything in the world.

26

*"Been a hustler since birth, mama sellin dinners for the church
Red-handed, caught me stealin money out her purse
Got branded, permanent whip scars on my back
Cause I used to get beat, with racing car tracks
But now me got wealth, holdin a conference call on my
hands free car telephone lookin like I'm talkin to myself."*

E-40

BLAME IT ON THE MUSIC

Artist: E-40

Album: The Element of Surprise (1998)

Hope I Don't Go Back

This song is classic from the legendary rapper E-40. He adds his unique style to it as he always does. Hope I Don't Go Back is a tale of a former drug dealer who became a very wealthy rapper. The story is one of reflection on the past, when life wasn't as easy and rewarding. I can't personally relate to the drug dealing part, but this story is very familiar. We have all been through experiences that we hope never take place again. E-40 tells this story so well that I can actually picture the events taking place. For some reason I instantly feel joy every time I hear this song. I've seen so many people fall victim to the street life, in my city (Detroit) it happens every day. I grew up around a bunch of drug dealers, thugs and killers. I've seen close childhood friends get caught up in these vicious cycles, I always promised myself that I would never take part. I felt like my life had a purpose and it wasn't to become another sad statistic. I lost a few people close to me to drugs and gun violence and those experiences taught me the dangers of traveling the wrong path. To me this song is so powerful because it's proof that a person can transition from a criminal to a successful businessman. It's a subject that needs more light shed upon it. I love the way E-40 says that you can leave the streets to make a better life for you and your family. I don't condone nor support selling drugs or partaking in violence, but I've been exposed to it my entire life. My message is that there are ways to transition out of the dangerous lifestyles. We need more people willing to help the lost souls, instead of judging and condemning them.

27

*"To the kids of the world that's waitin for wealth
Waitin for health, you better do for self
Homey that's yo last cup
Forget about the fast buck; boy, get yo ass up
People use yo brain to gain
Do something that ain't never been done; and we can spend hun's
Wipe our ass with twenties, light our joints with ones
Throw away the guns, have nothin but fun
And homey we could do that shit
Police have a fit, when yo paper's legit
We gotta get off the phone, we gotta teach our own
Send your baby to school and she'll come back grown
We got to talk to our grandmas
And she'll help us through them dark halls, and them pitfalls
Everybody know we got the world to gain
We got to stop the pain, Lord stop the rain."*

Ice Cube

BLAME IT ON THE MUSIC

Artist: Ice Cube and Krazie Bone

Album: War& Peace Vol.2: The Peace Disc (2000)

Until We Rich

The first time I heard this song, it spoke directly to me. I was 10 or 11 at the time, back then most songs I listened to weren't easy to comprehend. This actual book is a reflection of me having a better knowledge of the words that I sang along to when I was a kid. Krazie Bone and Ice Cube made this song for the young boys growing up in the ghetto. The two artists put together a confidence boosting track. The upbringings of young black boys are very challenging. We have to deal with a multitude of bullshit like absent fathers, mothers too young to be good parents, police brutality etc. **(I always felt disturbed when I heard Black parents tell their kids to be as non-threatening as possible around authority, which forces submission and passive behavior. I feel that some of our problems stem from being told what to do and who we are, instead of being encouraged to explore like the rest of the inhabitants of this world.)** These things usually happen before most young men have any say so in their lives. There's a disadvantage from birth, most are set-up to fail; obviously there's no room for excuses in life, but they exist. The world doesn't care that you grew up without a father, it doesn't matter if the cops profile you because of the color of your skin. Hearing this song lets us all know that life is too short to feed the negativity. Despite the odds not being in our favor, we all can make it past these obstacles. The solution is recognizing our own abilities, somedays it will feel like we don't stand a chance at

BLAME IT ON THE MUSIC

advancing in this world. I've seen people accept the fact that they will struggle for their entire life on earth. It takes a strong-willed, ambitious person to strive for a better future. It's too easy to feel trapped and become a victim; when you're accustomed to living a hard life, it all seems so routine. When these feelings are present change should be sought after, we are all creatures of habit. The habits don't discriminate either, good or bad ones are equally present. We must continue to strive to be Gods, life is meant to be experienced not just survived.

28

"I think that all the silence is worse than all the violence
Fear is such a weak emotion that's why I despise it
We scared of almost everything, afraid to even tell the truth
So scared of what you think of me, I'm scared of even telling you
Sometimes I'm like the only person I feel safe to tell it to
I'm locked inside a cell in me, I know that there's a jail in you
Consider this your bailing out, so take a breath, inhale a few
My screams is finally getting free, my thoughts is finally yelling through."

Lupe Fiasco

BLAME IT ON THE MUSIC

Artist: Lupe Fiasco

Album: Lasers (2011)

Words I Never Said

"When people don't express themselves, they die one piece at a time. You'd be shocked at how many adults are really dead inside-walking through their days with no idea who they are." Laurie Halse Anderson

What is fear? What really causes people to be quiet when they know they should speak up? How many times do we lack the confidence to say how we really feel? How many times do we ignore the opportunity to speak out about injustice? The power we possess with our words are enough to move mountains. On the other hand, our silence can be just as powerful. Many adults are full of regrets all because they were too afraid to express and verbalize how they felt. People lose their jobs and parents lose their children, all because some people aren't brave enough to speak up. Relationships are ended also because individuals are too stubborn or prideful to admit when they are wrong. I often complain about how bad my neighborhood looks. I'm learning that until I have the courage to do something about it, I have no right to complain about the conditions. When we express how we feel, good or bad, we start to create dialogue. Communication is the key to everything in life, we will continue to be doomed as long as we lack the ability to effectively communicate. Silence to the wrong thing can be just as bad as committing the act itself. Words I Never Said is relevant in every human's life. We are all given at least

BLAME IT ON THE MUSIC

one opportunity to say how we really feel. If you want to live a life full of regrets, then silence will assist you. The thing we all must remember is that we can't take back the words we never say.

BLAME IT ON THE MUSIC

29

"If the truth is told, the youth can grow
Then learn to survive until they gain control
Nobody says you have to be gangstas, hoes
Read more learn more, change the globe
Ghetto children, do your thing
Hold your head up, little man, you're a king
Young princess when you get your wedding ring
Your man is saying she's my queen."

Nas

BLAME IT ON THE MUSIC

Artist: Nas

Album: God's Son (2002)

I Can

I love the title of this song. In life we hear a lot of people telling us the things that we can't do. We're told what won't work and why we can't make certain things happen. Most of this doubt comes from adults who carry so many insecurities. They're filled with fear, regret and limited thinking. Most of these adults are stuck in a life that they hate, so they can't even imagine seeing others do any better. The perception of our environment can be another limiting factor, a lot of people never make it out of the ghetto. Some get out and end up going right back; it's all they know, the only place where they truly fit in. All of the doubts are true, you don't have to be a failure even if that's all you've been exposed to. Nobody has to accept their current circumstances if they don't want to. I Can is great song for those seeking confidence. We can do anything we set our hearts and minds to, the world is ours to gain. If you want something in life you have every right to pursue it, that doesn't mean that everything will go the way you like. We are the offspring of KINGS and QUEENS, we have the right to strive for and achieve greatness. I feel that not only do we have the right to, we should have an obligation to be great. We owe it to the children coming up behind us, we have to show them what hard work looks like. We have to show them what dedication, passion and persistence gets you. I am honored to share with my readers that we can be anything that we want to be, let's all strive to be amazing. We owe it to our ancestors and the generations

BLAME IT ON THE MUSIC

that follow us, all we have to do is believe. I KNOW I CAN, WHAT ABOUT YOU?

30

"Can I get a helping hand

Got a hand help me out

Immortality live it up

It took time but I'm finally getting out."

J Dove

BLAME IT ON THE MUSIC

Artist: J Dove

Album: Helping Hand (2014)

Helping Hand

One of the greatest things a person can do is assist someone else in a time of need. No matter how big or small that need is, everyone could use a little help. The amazing thing about helping someone is that the person lending a hand benefits as well. Cheerful givers are very rich people and I'm not talking about financial riches either. That's how we should all operate as human beings. If someone has a need that you can meet it should be done willingly; Sometimes greed and selfishness gets in the way. There's enough of everything on this planet for each human to be efficiently satisfied. It is tough to view it that way because most of us have been taught to accumulate as much as we can, even if we take from someone who needs it more. That creates scarcity and makes it seem like there's not enough to go around. Another reason someone might be reluctant to give is because some people lie and take advantage of willing givers. Believe it or not there are people who take advantage of kind hearted individuals; they make it hard for others that really do need a favor, all because they want a handout. We must all be aware of these sneaky individuals. This song title, Helping Hand, is a very fitting description of the artist who made it. J Dove is definitely one of the cheerful givers I spoke about earlier, he openly shares anything he has that can benefit others. I take pride in saying that I know this artist personally, he is my friend from High School and an overall amazing person. The amount of knowledge that he has given me can't be measured, I know that I'm not the only one who has benefitted from his willingness to stand out. From a personal standpoint, I often get inspired by seeing my peers succeed. So many of my friends have helped me believe in myself, all because they followed their dreams. Again this book is my way of giving back, I want to bless others the way this music and culture has blessed me. I hope that I've inspired the readers as much as these artists have inspired me.

31

"The streets robbed me, wasn't educated properly
Well fuck yall I needed money for Atari
Was so young my big sis still playin with Barbie
Young brother, big city, eight million stories
Old heads taught me, youngin, walk softly
Carry a big clip, that'll get niggaz off me
Keep coke in coffee, keep money smellin mothy
Change is cool to cop but more important is lawyer fees."

Jay-Z

BLAME IT ON THE MUSIC

Artist: Jay-Z

Album: The Blueprint (2001)

Never Change

Change is inevitable, whether we like it or not. In life we grow old, which isn't always a bad thing. There's rarely a period where no change is taking place. Progression should be welcomed, nobody wants to stay in the same position forever. Even when we're at our best, we all have room for improvements. Never Change is one of my favorite songs by Jay-Z. This song was from the street hustler and struggling rapper, a period where the artist had to say forget the industry. The song isn't the thoughts of a fifteen year chart topper and multi-million dollar company owner. He spoke of being too stubborn to change his ways, most street smart people share this exact same sentiment. They become so stuck in their ways that they refuse to grow. There's this unfortunate amount of pressure on blacks to remain the same when they start to experience success. We hear it all the time in the hood, a person is considered a sellout if they go out and create a better life for their selves and their family. The ironic part is that by staying the same we will continue to experience the things you want to get rid of. Losers don't become winners until they shift their mindset and their everyday actions. I used to cling to the rappers every word in this song. I felt a sense of pride, but I didn't understand the words that I spoke. I considered Jay-Z a sellout when the people around him faded from the spotlight, but he kept ascending. He reneged on his words in my mind. Since I've become an adult my mental capacity has increased. There's another hood mentality saying, it states that a person should shine with the people they struggled with, I agree with this statement to a certain extent. Sometimes circumstances shift and people who were once close drift apart. We should never stay around anyone because we feel obligated to, life is full of changes and we should embrace the chance to grow when the opportunity presents itself.

32

"Oh God how I love when the 1st come around
Now I'm feelin black and mild, headed cross town
Cause niggas the 1st to get celebrated
Rushin to the block cause I wanna get faded
Lookin all wild cause I'm getting me hair braided
We heavy off into this game
True to the 1st just call me that pro slang
Them nickels and dimes and 20's and 50's
The 1st be the day for the dope man."

Layzie Bone

BLAME IT ON THE MUSIC

Artist: Bone Thugs and Harmony

Album: E. 1999 Eternal (1995)

1st Of The Month

The ghetto holiday is the first of the month, anybody that has been on government assistance knows this all too well. Every month on this day the people receiving checks feel good, the difference can be noticed by anyone. Having money to spend is always a cause for celebration. The first is a good time for businesses in the hood, everything is usually crowded. I worked at McDonalds and Domino's pizza, the first and third days of each month were the busiest days every month. The only other time when people relentlessly spend their funds is during income tax season. People spend large amounts of money on fast food during these time periods. A lot of people who get checks regularly over indulge just because they can afford to. I find this quite disturbing, it makes me angry seeing my people spend uncontrollably. The problem is we all buy things that we want and neglect our basic needs. I'm not judging either, because I understand why it happens. We go without so much that when we're able to spend, we overdo it. Instead of building and creating we end up consuming and destroying all that we touch. Most people aren't taught any type of financial literacy, that's no excuse, but it is the truth. Blacks are allegedly the number one consumers in the United States, yet we're the most affected by poverty. This shows me that we need to become business owners and investors. How can we control so much capital and still suffer from a lack of resources and opportunities? The way unemployment is sky rocketing, now is the best time to take control of our finances. This would allow us to create solutions for the problems we face in our communities. Our goals should center on saving money and investing it.

33

"Diamonds on my hoes feet when they walk they spark
Diamonds in my fuckin teeth when I talk I spark
Don't fuck around with beef when it start, I spark
Me and my Hot Boy creeps when it's dark we spark
Just bought a new car, and I spent about a million
The motherfuckin driver seat sittin in the middle."

Baby

BLAME IT ON THE MUSIC

Artist: Big Tymers and The Hot Boys

Album: I Got That Work (2000)

#1 Stunna

When the Big Tymers and Cash Money first became mainstream, they were instantly popular. They made songs that made people want to party and just enjoy life. This song #1 Stunna was one of these party anthems, the group actually introduced the word stunna during this time. Taken from the word stunt, a stunna is someone who likes to show off. The Big Tymers were the ultimate show offs; they regularly bragged about how much money they had, their fancy cars and their plethora of expensive jewelry. I grew up around people who loved to flash their shiny jewels, cars, clothes and other material possessions. There is nothing wrong with having nice things and letting them be seen. The problem with stunting is that it can bring unwanted and unnecessary attention. When we seek approval and attention we fail to realize that instead of getting praise, we are welcoming envy and jealousy. It's disturbing to me that blacks too often use the material things in an attempt to make up for what they lack in other areas of their existence. We've been brainwashed to the point where we only place value upon perishable items. My people are stereotyped so much for being poor that we use any resort to escape poverty. We come from very rich backgrounds, before slavery our ancestors were rulers of the world. The dilemma is that we only value material riches which can come and go. Our focus should be on developing our intelligence, improving our health and sharing the love that we have in our hearts. This is not meant to be a critique towards the Big Tymers or the Hot

BLAME IT ON THE MUSIC

Boys I have respect for some of the things they accomplished. What I'm saying is that God has placed very unique gifts in each and every one of us. We can all shine bright and it will in return make this world a better place.

34

*"You had Elvis Presley and he was crackin
But guess what? Here comes Michael
Jackson
It's hood now
It's hood now
That's right
It's hood now
Pro sports, them was yo courts
But you let us in, so on and so forth
It's hood now
It's hood now."*

Lupe

BLAME IT ON THE MUSIC

Artist: Lupe Fiasco

Album: Food and Liquor 2 (2012)

Hood Now

Hood Now is a prideful song to me. I know that the odds are stacked against young blacks in the world, especially in this country. The world really tries to deny us every resource that will allow us to improve our circumstances. Despite the constant rejections and denials, we continue to persevere. We make a way out of nothing at all, this song really speaks on how we turn our adverse moments into statements. Whatever we touch, we leave our imprint. The entire world emulates us, even the people who repeatedly reject us. No matter what the situation is, we show up and we show out. Out of our despair we take average and make it extraordinary. The world's trash becomes our art; we set every trend that the world follows, good and bad. We go places we're not welcomed, we break barriers and set records in the process. Our words are used to make money, our thoughts become songs and movies. All the negativity we face is used to learn from it and use it to our advantage. We weren't allowed to play college or professional sports, look who's dominating almost every major sport in the world. Whatever we're given we somehow make the best out of it. I used to wonder why black people were rarely in the history books; sure we have a few talked about heroes, but ninety percent of the "greats" I studied were whites. This song actually explains it to anyone paying attention. There is a fear associated with black people in positions of power, we

BLAME IT ON THE MUSIC

would take over like we do in everything else. We wouldn't want the history books to be Hood Now, would we?

35

*"Some move away to make a way not move away cause they afraid.
I brought back to the hood and all you ever did was take away.
I pray for patience but they make me wanna melt their face away.
Like I once made them spray, now I could make them put the Ks away.
Been thuggin all my life, can't say I don't deserve to take a break
You'd rather see me catch a case, and watch my future fade away."*

T.I.

BLAME IT ON THE MUSIC

Artist: T.I. and Rihanna

Album: Paper Trail (2008)

Live Your Life

It is so easy to get distracted in life, we all have those times when we pay too much attention to things that don't concern us. I have seen a lot of people worried about another person's life, while they neglect their own problems. It's not easy to focus on your personal goals when you're caught up in what the next person is doing. One thing that is valued way too much is the opinion of other people, we have to stop caring what others think about us. Rapper T.I. is no stranger to controversy, he has his share of critics as well. No matter how many positive things a person does there will always be people who point out their faults and short-comings. Rihanna has also done some very questionable things with her large public spotlight as well, she is a huge role model for women all over the world. Her critics feel that she could be more conservative and conscious of the example that she's setting. Far too often we judge people who don't have the same views that we have. Our lifestyles vary and without the ability to walk in one another's shoes we can't really speak on anyone else's experiences. There are plenty of things that we all should be discussing taking action towards, but that shouldn't include gossiping about other people. Every individual human act impacts us all as a whole and once we start to realize that I think people will make better choices. Once we start to live with love and unity things will be better, but until that time comes **JUST LIVE YOUR LIFE!**

36

"You know that one auntie, you don't wanna be rude
But every holiday nobody eatin her food
And you don't wanna stay there cuz them your worst cousins
Got roaches at their crib like them your first cousins
Act like you ain't took a bath with your cousins
Fit three in the bed while six of y'all
I'm talkin bout three by the head and three by the leg
But you ain't have to tell my girl I used to pee in the bed."

Kanye West

BLAME IT ON THE MUSIC

Artist: Kanye West

Album: College Dropout (2004)

Family Business

No matter how many amazing people we encounter throughout our lives, no one can compare to our family. I'll admit, sometimes I become frustrated with members of my family; I've said harsh things to some of them as well. It's tough when you don't know your family's history, lacking any type of consistent traditions is what always angered me. My entire life up to this point has been spent longing for a close knit family. I can remember always being around my cousins, aunts and uncles growing up, but times have really changed. The sad part is that most of us live in the same city or within driving distance of one another. I miss the parties, get togethers and the times we all shared as kids and teens. I wish some things could have stayed the same, my family wasn't perfect but we used to enjoy one another's company. The world has changed so much since I was a kid and with those changes, obstacles and other problems have come as well. My family has lost loved ones that definitely held things together. I despise the fact that now it seems like my family, I'm sure my readers can relate, only comes together during times of tragedy. It's sad to only see your loved ones during funerals and/or hospital visits. It's terrible when you're struggling in any area of your life and you feel as if your family doesn't have your back. I've learned to accept the fact that some family members can be worse than strangers. I have also learned that family is not just relegated to your blood born relatives. True family members are those people

BLAME IT ON THE MUSIC

who are there for you no matter what. They are the people who aren't afraid to call you out when you're wrong and they'll celebrate your accomplishments with you as well. True family are the ones who want to see us become better people and live abundant lives.

37

"I'm just stating how I feel

And on the real for my brothers I would have killed

Everybody was eating like EBE, Chino was right about this movement

Stay Sucka Free."

FC Benji

BLAME IT ON THE MUSIC

Artist: FC Benji

Album: Off The Bench (2013)

Changed On Me

The more successful a person becomes, the more they attract envy from others. It is almost a guarantee that the better your life becomes, the more people will start to dislike you. Betrayal is a part of life, everyone goes through it at least once. One of the hardest parts of being crossed is that it usually comes from someone you're close to, this is especially true where I'm from. I know that sometimes people grow apart and stop being friends but sometimes there's an underlying issue. Jealousy is a real problem in this world, it creates division because of another person's insecurities. When someone starts to be in any type of spotlight, others tend to want that same attention. No matter how loyal a person claims to be, their actions will always be a true barometer. There's a saying, "you aren't growing up if you're not losing friends". I think that the older you get, the more you realize who your true friends really are. People will pretend to like you just to use you for their own gain. There are individuals who will love being around you when you have nothing to offer, then the moment you start to make progress in life, they turn their backs on you. Another group of people we can encounter are the ones who want to be around you when everything is going well, the moment you can't benefit them they disappear. Both groups are like wolves in sheep clothing, which makes it too tough to recognize their true intentions. These envious characters aren't limited to just friends either, family can be the most manipulative people ever. It's much easier for family to hide it, because you don't expect your relatives to cross you. Money is usually a huge reason why family and friends have turmoil, I've seen this my entire life. Any time a person becomes wealthy, everyone comes with their hands out. The wealthy one is looked at as a meal ticket and everyone feels entitled to share in their success, this makes it harder for them to trust anybody. My advice is don't put anything past anyone, allow people the opportunity to reveal their true selves and deal with them accordingly.

38

"And if you come from under that water then there's fresh air
Just breathe baby God's got a blessing to spare
Yes I know the process is so much stress
But it's the progress that feels the best
Cause I came from the projects straight to success and you're next
So try they can't steal your pride it's inside
Then find it and keep on grinding
Cause in every dark cloud there's a silver lining
I know."

Lil Wayne

BLAME IT ON THE MUSIC

Artist: Lil Wayne and Robin Thicke

Album: The Carter 3 (2008)

Tie My Hands

"After tragedy one has to be embraced", says famous author and poet Nikki Giovanni

August 25, 2005 Hurricane Katrina struck New Orleans, Louisiana. This national disaster really revealed a lot to anyone who was paying attention. The majority of the victims were poor people, particularly poor Black people. So many images were captured during the tragedy, there were pictures of little kids without any adults in sight. Survivors found anything they could to float on, dead bodies were everywhere. The town looked like a third world country in the aftermath, some survivors were stuffed in the Louisiana superdome. Cars and boats filled up the polluted streets. What I learned during this hurricane was that America didn't care about its poor black citizens, people were left to fend for their selves. Armed officers filled the streets denying the victims the ability to retrieve food from the ravished stores. CNN reporters called them refugees and they were treated as such; starving survivors were called looters, along with many other harsh names. The response from the government was very poor and too late. I have seen this country respond immediately to tragedies that struck other nations across the globe, they completely ignored Katrina victims. Lil Wayne is from the ghetto of New Orleans so this was a personal subject for him as well. He lost all of his material possessions, but unlike most of the poor survivors, he was

BLAME IT ON THE MUSIC

able to relocate and purchase more trinkets. I personally feel that there was a particular reason why relief efforts were poor and too late. I sympathize with everyone affected by Hurricane Katrina. Just like any other obstacles we've (Blacks) faced, those survivors bounced back and I applaud them for that.

39

"Prayin for young souls to laugh at life through the stars
Lovin your kids just like they was ours
And I'm hurtin for you dog; but ain't nobody pain is like yours
I just know that heaven'll open these doors
And ain't no bright side to losin life, but you can view it like this
God's got open hands homey, he in the midst of good company."

Scarface

BLAME IT ON THE MUSIC

Artist: Jay-Z and Scarface

Album: The Dynasty Roc La Familia (2000)

This Can't Be Life

This is a familiar tune in everyday living, from Detroit to every hood in the entire world. There are so many things that we deal with in our lives, so many obstacles to overcome. A lot of times in life, there are things that don't always work in our favor. We're equipped to lose most battles, which doesn't make us losers, we're just accustomed to the bad outcomes of most situations. The thing that I love about rap music is that it speaks for the hoods. There are things that go on every day in impoverished areas that never make the news, since its inception Rap has been our source of news. The music is the voice for the voice-less, even when we can't effectively verbalize our feelings, the music does it for us. Jay-Z, Scarface and Beanie Segal are all rappers who are more than qualified to speak for the ghettos. They all have come from these same streets, dealing with the everyday grind it takes just to get by. Survival is a trait that most of us adapt, it's the only way continue when the odds are against you. People have to make decisions that can lead to death or jail. Some may feel like they have no other choice, especially when the light company shuts your electricity off. Now that doesn't sound as bad as it really is, but try spending an entire winter without any heat or hot water. Adults and children have to deal with these type of conditions every day. Imagine having no food to feed your kids, I've felt like the artists in this song a lot in my life. The trauma and tragedy can make you think that you're living in hell. It can make you question God and

BLAME IT ON THE MUSIC

credit the devil for your hard times. Through it all though, life is what you make it, no matter what you go through. Your past doesn't have to hinder you, we all have to cherish where we came from and forge a new path.

BLAME IT ON THE MUSIC

40

"I see mothers in black cryin brothers in packs dyin
Plus everybody's high too doped up to ask why
Watchin our own downfall witness the end
It's like we don't believe in God cause we livin in sin."

Tupac Shakur

BLAME IT ON THE MUSIC

Artist: Tupac Shakur

Album: Better Dayz (2002)

Who Do You Believe In?

It can be difficult for believers with so many different religions in this world. This is especially true for young people who are trying to find their way in this world. With so many directions to go in, it becomes difficult to choose just one. Almost every person that has a religious background is following someone else. Some people just follow after their parents or the people who raised them. We all eventually make our own choices, but early on our decisions mirror our parent's choices. My parents weren't very religious when I was a child, my mom instilled basic Christian principles in me. I attended church in my younger years but I was rarely accompanied by my parents. I didn't know about God, I can't say that I believed all the doctrine I was taught either. My neighborhood was wild and chaotic back then and I didn't think that God cared about the people suffering there. At a young age I had seen so many tragedies, it seemed impossible to believe that Jesus actually saved people. I witnessed people who believed wholeheartedly get denied life's basic necessities. These life experiences caused me to be bitter towards God and religion in general. I also never liked the fact that most religions tried to recruit members to choose them, sort of like a cult. All these different choices just created further division amongst people. As a young adult I had some troubling experiences in a church that I had placed my trust in. Without going into detail I will say that I allowed the bad experiences to turn me away from God. I

BLAME IT ON THE MUSIC

refused to serve the same God as the people who hurt me, after years I learned that God had nothing to do with the actions of those individuals. I thought maybe God was protecting me by revealing things to me, I still have questions that will probably never be answered. Throughout it all I learned that I should focus on trusting and believing in myself above any person or religious organization.

41

*"Show me a God
I'm kinda feelin that it is a facade
Show me a God
And if it is, why ain't he doin his job
Show me a God
Even if it's a thing, a man, or a broad
Show me a God, please
Let me know something is listening when I'm down on my knees."*

Tech-9

BLAME IT ON THE MUSIC

Artist: Tech-9

Album: K.O.D. (2009)

Show Me a God

"Live by faith and not by sight." I grew up frequenting the church and around Christian people, I heard the quoted words a lot. I was taught at an early age to just believe in God, no questions asked. I also use to hear that God was everywhere all the time. In my younger days I did as I was told, which was to believe no questions asked, even when I was skeptical. The first time I can remember questioning the presence of God was on my thirteenth birthday, it was by far the worst day of my life. I woke up and found out that my mother had passed away. "God will never put more on you than you can handle", is another familiar saying I heard as an adolescent. My initial reaction was, why the hell does God think that I'm so tough? I felt it was no way that I could live the rest of my life without my mom. Then I wondered about my sisters; how could a God who was supposed to protect us just take our mother away? This made me question whether a god existed at all. I had my reasons too, I was a devastated teenager. Other believers asked me who was I to question God, I felt bad and just dealt with the pain. I always found it hysterical how so called Christians tried to guilt trip others into believing their personal beliefs. All of the questions that I had back then have started to resurface now that I'm an adult. The difference now is that I don't feel bad questioning religion or anything else. With so many religions around the world, I wonder who God really is. I heard that we were made in the image of the lord, does that make us God? I'm

BLAME IT ON THE MUSIC

far from a non-believer, I just recognize that when I'm staring in the mirror, I'm staring into the eyes of God and so are you.

BLAME IT ON THE MUSIC

42

"At 18 I was stressing, I'm diagnosed with depression

Every time she say she love me then I started second guessing

Cause the man up in the mirror ain't never showed affection

And I'm scared to fall asleep because there's someone after me."

Chino

BLAME IT ON THE MUSIC

Artist: SFC Chino

Album: LSD (2014)

Suicide

When I was a young boy I always wondered what caused people to take their own lives. Suicide has always been a mystery to me, what could be so bad that living was no longer an option? While it is a tough subject to address, suicide is something that should be talked about more. I've heard people call it cowardice and selfish to take your own life, I feel that it is a result of unanswered cries for help. It's easy to blame the person committing the act; the thing that most aren't willing to address is the reasons behind the acts and ways to prevent them. Obviously no one can speak for an individual that is no longer alive. So instead of condemning anyone to hell, we should contribute to the awareness of the obstacles that most of us face. I'm presenting this song with pride because my longtime friend is the one who created it. I can tell that this is a personal issue that he dealt with. It takes courage to admit that life has gotten the best of you, especially as a man. Too often we keep our feelings suppressed until it's too late to fix them. People also turn to drugs, alcohol, violence, etc... to numb the pain that they're dealing with. It is not easy living in this world and there are people going through challenging times. I have had times in my life when I felt like I would be better off dead, I eventually erased those feelings. My negative thoughts stemmed from not understanding my purpose on this earth. When a person places value on their life, they are confident and aware that they are needed here on earth. I feel

BLAME IT ON THE MUSIC

that as people we should value each other a lot more, in return we will all feel needed and cherished as well.

43

*"I done teached and talked
Walked away and fought
Went from cussin and bustin
Hustle from day to dark
Turned nothin to somethin
Introduced to stunning."*

Mannie Fresh

BLAME IT ON THE MUSIC

Artist: Big Tymers and the Hot Boyz

Album: I Got That Work (2000)

My Life

I didn't even own this album, my boy John Webb let me borrow it. I wanted it because I wanted to listen to #1 Stunna and Get Your Roll On. After listening to the entire album this song stood out to me the most, I loved the story telling and the nice beat. It took me about a week to give John his cd back, this was before the arrival of cell phone music, Ipods and mp3 players. My Life reminded me that everyone has a story to tell, I love to sit back and listen to people tell me stories from their past. They talk about things they used to be good at and things they always wanted to experience. My Life is a testament to the fact that we're all human and we all have hopes, dreams and aspirations. I have been through a few devastating things in my life. I wasn't even eleven years old when my uncle laid in a hospital bed and told my big sister and me that he was HIV positive. Despite his optimism we could see that he was on his death bed. I watched helplessly as my best friend and his sister had to bury their father, not knowing a few years later it would be me and my sisters painfully watching as our mother laid in a casket. Even though it has been thirteen years since that day, the pain of losing my mom never ceased. I still can't understand the reasoning behind some of the obstacles that I have been through. In this song there's a message to *"tell yo mama you love her before she dead and gone"*. I can remember repeating those words over and over in my head as a twelve year old, even when the song wasn't playing. I'm

BLAME IT ON THE MUSIC

filled with guilt to this day because I didn't listen when I still had the chance. I urge my readers to show love to your family while they're still alive. One thing we have to do after people pass away is keep on living our lives. We have to do everything in our power to make our loved ones proud. I'm filled with optimism because I know my life is improving everyday despite the pain I've endured. There's hope in each breath we're given so I plead with everyone to enjoy your life and count your blessings.

44

*"I'm ready to meet him
Where I'm living ain't right
Black hate white
White hate black
It's right back
To the same fight
They got us suspecting a war
But the real war is to follow the law of the lord."*

DMX

BLAME IT ON THE MUSIC

Artist: DMX

Album: Flesh of My Flesh, Blood of My Blood (1998)

Ready To Meet Him

If you've ever felt so overwhelmed with life that you were ready to die, then this song will speak to you. DMX is an artist who pours his heart out in his music, he goes places and speaks on subjects that other artists wouldn't dare. As a teen every time, I heard this track I instantly became afraid. Now that I'm older I can relate to the lyrics, life can be such a roller coaster. There are so many ups, as well as so many downs. Even the strongest people have periods where they might just want to throw in the towel. This world can be so cold, sometimes we just want a release from the everyday trouble that we encounter. No one is immune to those dark destructive thoughts of death, it's up to the individual on how they choose to deal with these thoughts. I've seen people resort to destructive behavior as a method to deal with life's stresses. Alcohol abuse is one of those ways that people attempt to escape reality. It's not a good coping mechanism, because once the liquor wears off the problems still exist. In most ghetto neighborhoods, alcohol and drug use are a part of everyday life. They are as routine as brushing your teeth to some. I'm not saying it's the right way to cope, but it happens regularly. Personally I don't like resorting to either while I'm dealing with the hardships life has to offer me. I have seen so many people become addicts in my short lifetime. I feel that one of my life's purposes is to help people overcome their dark days. I hope that doing what I'm good at

BLAME IT ON THE MUSIC

is an inspiration for others to seek a positive outlet to all the madness.

BLAME IT ON THE MUSIC

45

*"Wishin death on other nigga's mothers ain't right but why mommy
She raised me in the projects alone
Her untimely exit from her, heavenly body
Got me ready to body somethin quickly
Can't be happy, fuck a party she can't party with me
So your apologies are burnin ya own souls
To the kids with no parents at home, grab a hold."*

Nas

BLAME IT ON THE MUSIC

Artist: Nas and Alicia Keys

Album: God's Son (2002)

Warrior Song

This song's title is very self-explanatory. The definition of a warrior according to The American Heritage dictionary, is a person engaged in some struggle or conflict. There are so many individuals who can call their selves warriors. Almost every living being is engaged in some type of struggle or conflict. No matter how big or small these struggles are, we all face them. I feel like most of my life has been a big struggle, I've been faced with countless opportunities to give up. Out of all the struggle and pain, champions are bred. If you channel your energy, the hurt can and will make you a stronger person. I actually take pride in knowing that I can handle very difficult situations. I'm a true survivor of many obstacles, I think that I'm battle tested. If you have been through anything and you're still alive to talk about it, then you are a warrior too. To be classified as a true warrior you have to be willing to fight; not just physical battles and it should always be a worthy cause. It takes very heroic men and women to fight on others' behalf. Guys like Marcus Garvey, Huey P. Newton, Nat Turner, Malcolm X and Martin Luther King Jr fit the warrior description; as well as women like Afeni Shakur, Harriet Tubman, Rosa Parks and Assata Shakur. All of the individuals that I named exemplify these characteristics, they were willing to take on battles for the sake of their people as a whole. They never gave up, even if it meant they would die in the process. They all knew that even in death they were fighting for something greater

BLAME IT ON THE MUSIC

than themselves. If everyday people adopted the mindsets of the previously mentioned greats, we would rule the world. It's time that we learn from our ancestors and become true warriors. I want to encourage my readers no matter what battle you are facing, never give up!

46

"What can I say to him? I'm determined to pray for him Father empty and break him I pray you'll just have your way with him, cuz there's a change in him and the effects are strong, I pray you open up his heart before the next song and when he gets home, I pray he'll open up the sixty-six book love letter you wrote and soak it up cuz he ain't hearin You and he ain't feelin me and God I know it's killin You because it's killin me and matter of fact there's somethin else he's concealin see, the person that I've been prayin about is really me."

Lecrae

BLAME IT ON THE MUSIC

Artist: Lecrae

Album: After The Music Stops (2006)

Praying for You

In church believers are taught to pray for their selves as well as others. We pray for things we want to receive and for the things we want to keep. Praying is viewed as our direct communication with the creator himself. When life seems overwhelming and chaotic, prayer is our opportunity to vent and discuss our lives. Over a great beat Lecrae lays outs his thoughts, I love the way he wasn't afraid to show vulnerability. We all go through periods where we feel like failures, there's times when we think negative and feel frustrated. I can personally relate to this song, I have got caught up in everyday troubles before. I've allowed my mind to create worst case scenarios that weren't always realistic. During those despairing moments I often forgot the comfort that praying provides. It allows us to have alone time with our thoughts and with God. When we seek guidance, we're often instructed to just read the Bible or our holy books. The problem with that is they just give us information, most of the stuff we already know. The stillness of prayer is something that can only occur in the act itself. Praying helps bring our thoughts, emotions and frustrations to the present, when we express these things our burdens can be lifted. Lord knows we all need lighter loads to carry throughout life. Personally this past year has been quite demanding for me and my loved ones. We've had to say goodbye to young adults far too soon. Obviously it's a part of being adults, but it is very hard to deal with. Just as much as we pray during

BLAME IT ON THE MUSIC

our challenging times we should also pray amongst our triumphs. We have to be grateful for life when everything is going good as well as when things seem overwhelming and prayer can help us accomplish that.

47

"I'm giving you a wakeup call
Wake up, wake up
Just to say that I love you
And that I'm thinking of you
Lettin you know that you got friends

I'm giving you a wakeup call
Wake up, wake up
It's a beautiful day
Don't let it slip away
And live it like it's the first day
Of the *rest of your life."*

Ke Ke Palmer

BLAME IT ON THE MUSIC

Artist: Ke Ke Palmer

Album: So Uncool (2007)

Wake-Up Call

I think that everyone gets excited or feels good when someone calls just to see how they're doing, I rarely receive phone calls like this. Most calls I get are from people asking me for money or to do them a favor. I used to feel good being the guy that my family and friends called when they needed help. It started to become overwhelming because I started to feel like they were using me. When I couldn't come to their aid immediately the calls ceased, some people will take advantage of you if you allow them to. Despite being an amazing actress, Ke Ke Palmer is a music artist as well. I don't normally listen to Disney star's music, but I'm glad that I heard Wake Up Call. This song reminds me of lifes' carefree days; the days when nothing really mattered and having fun was the only objective. I miss the joy of being a kid and not having any major responsibilities. Despite this song being for young teens, Wake Up Call can be enjoyed by adults as well. On the days where life seems stressful and overwhelming, we should all be happy that we woke up. We have to embrace the fact that we are still alive, life is very precious and we shouldn't take it for granted. Along with accepting our tasks in life we must learn to live with purpose and cheer. Every day won't be easy, but we must overcome the rough days. I encourage all of my readers to look around and embrace how beautiful your lives are and call someone you love just to check on them.

48

*"And I can't even go to the grocery store
Without some ones that's clean and a shirt
with a team
It seems we living the American dream
But the people highest up got the lowest self-
esteem
The prettiest people do the ugliest things
For the road to riches and diamond rings
We shine because they hate us, floss cause
they degrade us
We trying to buy back our 40 acres."*

Kanye West

BLAME IT ON THE MUSIC

Artist: Kanye West

Album: College Dropout (2004)

All Falls Down

I previously spoke about financial literacy in the ghetto communities, we all have this internal need to show what we're worth. It's all too familiar in the hoods everywhere, most people try to be flashy. In the summer there's so many cars with the big and shiny rims on them, jewelry is worn as personal enhancements. With the emergence of social media it has become more complex, we're now able to edit and filter our photos and ultimately our lives. This world has become so strange, low self-esteem is at the center of this epidemic. A person who thinks highly of their self doesn't need the validation from the rest of the world. The problem is that most of us have only been reminded of the areas where we fall short; instead of focusing on our strengths, we attempt to be something that we're not. Kanye spoke about this lack of confidence in All Falls Down, the honesty in his music is what makes him such an influential person. He didn't shy away from his inner feelings, which is a major deterrent amongst all humans. Instead of admitting how we feel, we try to hide our feelings. We become unaware that our actions are a reflection of our feelings and insecurities. I never understood why people brag about the things that they wear, this is common in my city. People are so brand happy, which isn't a bad thing; to me it's a problem when we degrade others who don't own particular expensive items. Money makes you more valuable in the eyes of most people in today's society. Some individuals vouch so much for certain brands, you would think that they created them. In my eyes the more money I save, the more I'm worth financially. The producers want to convince us that the more we spend is how we measure our worth. True self-worth has nothing to do with a dollar amount or purchasing power. Our eyes can really deceive us if we allow them to. A goal of all humans, black people especially, should be to gain confidence in ourselves. We have to start looking within for the things we seek externally. When we become genuine and feel worthy with who we were created to be, the world will benefit as a result.

BLAME IT ON THE MUSIC

49

"I'm in the club every night you a homebody

Throwin bands by myself at my own party

Celebrating bout the wealth cuz I'm on finally

And I'm with two thick bitches that's on Molly."

Vezzo

BLAME IT ON THE MUSIC

Artist: Icewear Vezzo

Album: The Clarity 2 (2013)

Thick Bitch

In each of us there lies a duality. I wasn't going to include this song for obvious reasons, but I had to. Music doesn't have to always be so serious and stern. I'll admit I love hearing uplifting, motivating music most of the time. I'm also a twenty-seven year old male and I have my faults as well. Some will say that ignorance in music is the problem, I once felt this way. One of the problems is that we scrutinize others so much more than we judge ourselves. Music is art and a form of creative expression; the world would rather censor artists, which is unrealistic. Coming from Detroit, I understand that my views and values are different from a person in another city. The artists from the ghetto are often viewed as negative, but most of them are just speaking on what they've witnessed in their life. Good or bad, I feel that it is the artists' right to share their experiences. This song title is very controversial, but most rap songs are. Detroit's very own Icewear Vezzo just voiced some men's preference in women, someone who is thick and curvy. I like all different types of women, but I love to see a lady with a nice looking body. It's unfair to the young women who strive to be wanted just because of the shape of their body. It causes some of them to attempt to become the prototype on the outside, ignoring the need to cultivate the person on the inside. The latter is true for men and women alike. Another critique about this song could be the word that a lot of women hate, bitch. The word is viewed as less lethal in this song because he's saying thick bitch. I'm not attempting to argue the context in which it's used, I just think that this is a good song that we can all vibe to. I can relate to him because I love thick women too.

50

"Just like that, you see the fruit of the confusion
He caught in a reality, she caught in an illusion
Bad mean good to her, she really nice and smart
But bad mean bad to him, bitch don't play a part
But bitch still bad to her if you say it the wrong way
But she think she a bitch, what a double entendre."

Lupe Fiasco

BLAME IT ON THE MUSIC

Artist: Lupe Fiasco

Album: Food and Liquor 2 (2012)

Bitch Bad

The word Bitch can mean so much, it's usually used out of context. I was told that it described a female dog, but I rarely heard it when people talked about their dogs. Every time I heard the vulgar word, it was directed towards a woman. The use of the word bitch is a difficult topic to address. I have seen women fight men for calling them a bitch. I regularly hear women refer to their close friends with the term, I know men who will harm anybody who uses it to describe them. The reason is that it's viewed as a feminine word and it emasculates men. When it comes to the ladies it just a matter of who's saying it and how they're saying it. In today's culture putting the word bad in front of bitch creates a different twist to the word; it then ironically becomes a term of endearment and flattery. Even though bad isn't a positive word, it is when you put it before bitch. A Bad Bitch is supposed to mean the best looking woman, I'll admit I have used this phrase to describe a nice looking woman. Sometimes I say it with ease and without second thought, other times I say it and feel shame. When I actually called female dogs bitches, people usually got mad; that has always been confusing to me. Saying bitch with anger could also display disrespect but if it's said politely some people still get mad. Bad Bitch is used by people of this generation to describe beautiful women, most of the time. Lupe created a few scenarios in this song that makes you think, the different instances just give me more questions. Bitch Bad is a great

BLAME IT ON THE MUSIC

way to create dialogue; the word bitch causes a lot of misunderstanding, so I will try my best not to use it at all.

51

*"Thinkin how they spend 30 million dollars
on airplanes
When there's kids starvin
Pac is gone and Brendas still throwin babies
in the garbage
I wanna know what's goin on like I hear
Marvin
No school books they use that wood to build
coffins
Whenever I'm in the booth and I get
exhausted
I think what if Marie Banker got that abortion
I love you Ma."*

The Game

BLAME IT ON THE MUSIC

Artist: The Game and G-Unit

Album: The Documentary (2005)

Hate It or Love It

Rooting for the underdog is a popular thing to do for a lot of people. It's because we can directly identify with them, I know I personally can. My entire life I've been told why I wasn't good enough; to someone I was always too short, too skinny, too black, too dumb, etc... As a young man I started to believe the doubts that others had about me, which caused me to disregard the beliefs I should have had in myself. I've given up on things that I really wanted just listening to outsiders. I feel like I would be much better in my life if I had always believed in myself. Where I'm from the expectations are really low, especially for black men. I didn't learn the value of setting goals until I was a full grown adult, so every achievement I had was viewed as a success and not a stepping stone. What I mean is due to the low expectations I never strived to build on my latest accomplishment. This behavior made me become complacent, I didn't take control of my life I just went along with the flow. I have seen so many other people do this as well. When we don't strive for anything, we undervalue our lives. As a teen I pointed my finger, blaming others; my parents weren't together, the coach doesn't like me, the teacher always singles me out. When reality sets in there is no room for excuses, I had to learn how to hold myself accountable. My success depended on me and only me, adopting that attitude helped me tremendously. I no longer use where I'm from as an excuse for failure, I decided to use it as motivation. I couldn't let my

BLAME IT ON THE MUSIC

mother's death hold me back, as bad as it hurts, it now fuels me. The climb to the top for me is so rewarding because I've seen the bottom before. My advice would be to let go of all the reasons you can't do the things you dream of; focus on why you can, work hard and you will receive everything that you deserve.

52

*"So many years of depression make me vision
The better living, type of place to raise kids in
Open they eyes to the lies history's told foul
But I'm as wise as the old owl, plus the gold child
Seeing things like I was controlling, click rolling
Tricking six digits on kicks and still holding
Trips to Paris, I civilized every savage
Gimme one shot I turn trife life to lavish."*

Nas

BLAME IT ON THE MUSIC

Artist: Nas and Lauryn Hill

Album: It Was Written (1996)

If I Ruled The World

I want you to sit back and imagine how it would be if we all lived harmoniously. Think about people helping each other, bartering and just complimenting one another. What if racism didn't exist? How much different would this world be? I wonder what a planet void of greed and selfishness looks like. We all know that nothing is perfect, but that doesn't mean we can't dream. Two of the most conscious artists collaborated on this song. If I Ruled The World is a very fitting title for a song that has Nas and Lauyrn Hill on it. Both of these artist remind blacks that we are royalty, Kings and Queens are supposed to rule. It's very important to reiterate that we (blacks) are the descendants of Kings and Queens. Even though the things we were taught display us as slaves and the scum of the earth. Most people would find it hard to believe, especially in the hood, that blacks are anything other than savages and bottom feeders. It's very frustrating to be treated and viewed like you're not even a human being. If you're worth little money your life is viewed as less important, that's a sad reality that all poor people face. This is true for all humans despite their race and nationality. It creates a life where people just chase after meaningless things because they feel worthless. We ignore our true gifts and live less fulfilling lives. If I ruled the world there wouldn't be a deliberate attempt to make a certain race inferior. I would require everyone to obtain high self-esteem also creativity and individuality would be encouraged. A far-fetched as it sounds, each individual on this planet is a ruler. We have the power to control and direct our own lives, recognizing this power will allow us to see endless possibilities.

BLAME IT ON THE MUSIC

53

*"Yep yep that's my word
Make a statement with these nouns and verbs
I represent the liquor that's poured out on the curb
Listen to my nouns and verbs man I wanna be heard
Like a cattle with sheep
While yall sleep I be up, cooking up all day like a mad scientist in that laboratory
Motherfuck what a critic got to say, I'm a be heard."*

Kendrick Lamar

BLAME IT ON THE MUSIC

Artist: Kendrick Lamar

Album: Kendrick Lamar EP (2009)

Wanna Be Heard

The many stages that we go through in life can leave us searching for our identity. A lot of people spend their youth following trends and mimicking others. It's so much power when you find out who you really are. In this world individuality is often frowned upon, but when people discover their true selves they ought to spend the rest of their lives displaying it. Wanna Be Heard speaks on things that most people think; most of us think that we have something to offer the world, we all at least have a story to tell. Everyone wants that attention, we all want to be heard by someone we can help or someone who can assist us. We all want to feel like our opinions matter in all that we experience. That's why rappers/artists are so influential, most of them can identify with people. We all have at least one song that we feel was made exactly for us. Entertainers get to say what normal people are afraid to say, it's a relief hearing someone else speak about experiences that we have gone through. Wanna Be Heard was written for me at my current position in life, there's a voice on the inside of me screaming and yelling to be unleashed. The world needs to hear this voice but I've had a tough time letting it out. I'm sure that I can't be the only person facing this battle, I'm trying to find my place in this world we live in. I'm trying to convince myself that I'm worthy and that what I have to say really matters. I want to have the confidence to know that my opinion really does count, it's safe to say I want the world to

BLAME IT ON THE MUSIC

hear me out. Thank you Kendrick Lamar for giving me the courage to share some of my inner most thoughts with everyone.

54

"This fuckin job can't help him
So I quit, yall welcome
Yall don't know my struggle
Yall can't match my hustle
You can't catch my hustle
You can't fathom my love dude
Lock yourself in a room doin five beats a day
for three summers
That's a different world like Kree Summers
I deserve to do these numbers."

Kanye West

BLAME IT ON THE MUSIC

Artist: Kanye West

Album: College Dropout (2004)

Spaceship

When Kanye first became a famous rapper he was like a savior of music. His songs were so real and they were something a lot of people could identify with. I heard Spaceship before I had a real job, my first gig as an adult was at McDonalds. I was so embarrassed to tell anyone that I worked there. All the jokes I heard about dead-end jobs were all directed at McDonalds. I felt like a complete failure, because a year earlier I was a student at Michigan State University. I want you to imagine what it feels like to drop out of your dream school only to end up working a graveyard shift. Initially I was happy to finally be able to provide for myself, it wasn't much because minimum wage was like six dollars at the time. I found it quite amusing when longer tenured employees bragged to me about making twenty cents more than the minimum, I guess that made them feel more important. I just felt out of place, I knew that I didn't belong there. I won't act like all I had was bad times though, because working at the McDonalds on 7mile and Gratiot was like its own reality show. I experienced almost everything there, except getting robbed thank God. The biggest thing that I gained from being employed there was becoming more humble. I never thought that normal people worked at fast-food restaurants. In my mind the places were full of high school dropouts and people who couldn't do any better in life. I ended up working there for approximately three years, I used to be so embarrassed when I saw people I knew

BLAME IT ON THE MUSIC

buying food. I felt ashamed and thought they would think less of me, but all they cared about was getting a free pop or some more french fries. I barely got any type of raises despite being a hard worker, I felt like a paid slave. I contemplated quitting so many times. It wasn't until I had grown tired of the constant threats of getting fired, that I just decided to never go back again. Plus I had woke up late so I would have got fired anyways, but that's not the point. People told me don't quit without a backup plan or without putting in two weeks' notice. (I always felt putting in a notice of quitting at certain places was sort of pointless. All they would do is give you less days which would defeat the purpose.) I recognized that most people would put up with unfair treatment, unequal pay and borderline slavery for minimum wage jobs. Not me though, I refuse to allow a job the power to destroy my will to be great, I rather have less money short- term and keep pursuing my dreams.

BLAME IT ON THE MUSIC

55

"My heart is full of rage

Enemies they portray me as thangs in the cage.

Backs turned for ReNisha hoodies on for the Trayvon."

Che

BLAME IT ON THE MUSIC

Artist: Detroit Che

Album: None

Life Span

Detroit Che is another artist that I started following on Instagram. I didn't really know how talented of a rapper she was until later on, but I loved the way she used her platform to speak out on social issues. I was outraged when I heard the tragic story about Renisha McBride on the news. November 2, 2013 a nineteen year old black woman was shot and killed by a white male while she was seeking help after a car accident. The story made national news and was one of the many stories of a black person being shot and killed by a white person. Life Span is a song made in the memory of Renisha McBride, Trayvon Martin and the many others whose life was cut short due to fear, hatred and complete negligence. Despite what most people are willing to admit, black lives aren't treated with value in this country. As a black man I can say that we see no value in each other and neither does any other race, in my opinion. This is not me speaking ignorantly, these are well known truths. We've watched cops, racists, thugs and many more hatred filled beings assassinate black people without facing any major consequences. It's as if we're viewed as insignificant, so we get used until we can't be exploited any longer. People talk about how far we've come and how much things have changed, to me that's all up for debate. In the past few years alone, there have been some sad revelations about blacks in America. Prior to Trayvon Martin's death, I had never heard of the stand your ground law. The law has protected whites who have murdered blacks because they were intimidated and/or afraid of their presence. It starts from a prejudice that all blacks are violent and looking to cause trouble. The harsh truth is that we're not expected to live long prosperous lives. The counter argument keeps coming up about how blacks kill each other all the time, which is true. The problem is that a black person will get buried under the jail when they murder anyone and get caught but there aren't many consequences when another race murders us. I feel that any time murders are used to justify other killings, there is a serious problem going on. There seems to be an agenda in place that continuously makes it tougher for blacks to prosper. I see why the schools in Detroit, and all predominately black neighborhoods, don't receive the proper help from the government. I now realize why young black men are sentenced as adults and sent to prison immediately. Majority of the world would probably say that the person pointing out these truths are racist, I wish I was making these things up. I'm not a racist and I feel no need to further explain, what I am is unapologetically BLACK. I refuse to allow other people's image of me to persuade me to change who I am; I embrace the person that God created me to be and I hope you do as well.

56

*"This the road life we live and aint nobody stopping
it's either get the bag or go get a job mopping
So who got em cause I'm out shopping
I don't see me working 8 hours for 7 dollaz."*

Peezy

BLAME IT ON THE MUSIC

Artist: Team Eastside Peezy

Album: Mud Muzik (2014)

Out The Hood

Every time this song comes on I feel a sense of urgency; making it out the hood has always been one of my dreams. I say dream instead of goal because I never even thought about the type of life I would have outside of the ghetto. I was born and raised in some of the worst neighborhoods in the city of Detroit. I've always heard rappers and entertainers speaking about escaping the hoods that they grew up in. It's sad to think about because the conditions have to be horrendous for everyone to want to escape them. The more I think about it, the more revealing the truth becomes; there is no escaping the ghetto. No matter how far you move away, or how much better your life becomes, there is no way to completely leave. I'm not saying that a better lifestyle and safer surroundings shouldn't be sought after. The dilemma to me is that these places (hoods/ghettos) will always exist until the people that understand them the most take serious initiative to improve the conditions. Of course it sounds impossible and I'm sure many have tried, but it must be done. I once heard that a hood is something that's used to hide something else. The world has tried to hide the ghetto for far too long. One of the reasons I feel that there's no escaping is the fact that we all have family and close friends here, I feel obligated to help pull them out as well. I wish life didn't have to be this way, I wish we all had it a little easier. Instead of complaining, sulking and blaming others we must unite and create neighborhoods and communities that we don't want to escape from.

57

*"Where's my gangstas and all my thugs
Throw them hands up and show some love
And I welcome you to Detroit City
I said welcome to Detroit City
Every place, everywhere we go
Man we deep everywhere we roll
Ask around and they all know Tricky
Ask what's good man they all say Tricky."*

Eminem

BLAME IT ON THE MUSIC

Artist: Eminem and Trick Trick

Album: None

Welcome to Detroit

Detroit is a city full of hard workers, only the strong survive in this town. Detroit has a rich History of both devastating times and triumphant ones. Some of the most famous people in the world were born here or lived here. I often visualize how vibrant this city was when Motown was the center of the music business. It wasn't a shock for you to get to see The Temptations, Michael Jackson or Diana Ross at any time of the day. I wish I was alive during those days, I heard so many positive stories. Detroit was famous for all the right reasons; as we all know times have changed. The city I'm familiar with is drastically different from back in the day. People around the world only hear about our high crime rates, abandoned homes and high unemployment. Nothing is shocking to the people that live here, we all know that anything can happen at any time. The inner city neighborhoods resemble a war zone. With all the negative news available about this city, one would think that all hope is lost. That's where the entire world is wrong, there are some exciting things going on here in Motown. The youth have been struck with a sense of purpose and direction. Anyone really paying attention can see the momentum shifting in the favor of the people here. This is especially true on the music scene, despite a few incidents along the way. There is a plethora of talented individuals in my hometown. The thing I take pride in is seeing everyone start to unite. We all know about the eastside versus west side crap that has plagued us

BLAME IT ON THE MUSIC

for too long. It's safe to say that that is a thing of the past, thanks to Tommy Walker it's now Detroit versus Everybody.

58

"Me and rappers don't get along fuck yall

they ask me do I think Trick was wrong, Fuck naw

That's the only one I see sticking up for us how he gone fuck it up for us

They already don't fuck with us."

Helluva

BLAME IT ON THE MUSIC

Artist: Various Local Detroit Artists

Album: none (2014)

Detroit Over Everything

Friday November 28, 2014 history was made in the city of Detroit. Aside from the fact that it is a great song, this track means more than music alone. Some of the attitudes of people in this city are no different than other places in the world. You have these people who barely own anything being so territorial, it's always been unnecessary competition amongst people of the city. I know you've heard of the eastside versus west side beefs, we even have six mile versus seven mile beef; it reminds me of someone describing the days of slavery when there were bouts between the house slaves and the field slaves. What I'm trying to say is that there has never been a time where people of this city has set aside their differences and came together for a greater purpose, at least not in my lifetime. I sat in my room and waited for part one of this song to debut on the radio and as I listened to some of the artist talk about the reasons behind this music, it made me rejoice. If you've watched any type of news or media outlets it has painted a bad picture of Detroit. It's safe to say that the world doesn't like us; I'm not talking about downtown or Metro Detroit where things are a little safer, I'm speaking about the hoods. We've had a few instances where our bad reputation has been warranted. On the music side, I wish Blade and Wipeout were alive to see this. Lives have been lost right here in this city because people were too stubborn to set their pride aside. I salute all the artists for agreeing to come together for something

BLAME IT ON THE MUSIC

greater than their personal differences. It has always been an us versus the world mentality as far as music goes in this city. We're usually overlooked, so when Detroit versus Everybody was introduced to the world, it solidified our stance. Unity should be embraced amongst all humans, there's no better place to start than in your own backyard. I'm so excited to see what this movement will spark in the city. Even though I had nothing to do with these collaborations, I'm filled with pride because finally it's Detroit Over Everything.

BLAME IT ON THE MUSIC

59

*"Now that I'm grown, I got my mind on bein somethin
Don't wanna be another statistic, out here doin nothin
Tryin to maintain in this dirty game, keep it real
and I will even if it kills me, my young niggaz break away from these dumb niggaz."*

Tupac Shakur

BLAME IT ON THE MUSIC

Artist: Tupac Shakur

Album: Me Against The World (1995)

Young Niggaz

As a child I didn't realize how much the odds were stacked against me. When I was coming up most young black boys maintained their innocence, just like the other kids. It is extremely tough for young men to grow up in the ghetto, I'm from the hood and it wasn't easy. Every day the threat of getting hit with a stray bullet was a possibility. I have been threatened with gun violence on plenty of occasions, simply playing basketball. Witnessing drug deals became acceptable at young age for me and my peers. Most of the children grow up in homes without a strong male setting the proper examples. This creates voids in most lives and the streets are often there to fill that emptiness. I've seen people get so caught up in a negative lifestyle that they can't escape the traps that the streets offer. This is a trend that has to be discontinued, before we're all wiped out. Despite his thug persona Tupac Shakur was an advocate for young black males. In this song he reflects on the way most boys from the ghetto are raised. We see the status and money that the drug dealers get and we want to emulate them. The poor living conditions make you resort to any method to get money. Unfortunately most people who become addicted to the fast life can't escape, death and jail become two of the most likely destinations. When I was about fifteen I had a lot of young guys who looked up to me, I always made sure that I was a positive influence on them as a result. I feel guilty now because most of these guys are now adults and they're living

BLAME IT ON THE MUSIC

a fast life. It makes me feel like I failed all these young men. I put enormous pressure on myself to help lead these men on a positive path and I neglected my responsibilities as I grew older. I haven't lost hope for any of those guys, but I wish I knew back then what I know now. I will use every day that I have left in this physical body to assist kids that everyone else would rather give up on, Tupac was on that mission before he passed away. In the song he urges the boys to put down the guns and have fun; he also said they should aspire to be something greater than entertainers and street hustlers. I just want to spread the message and tell these young men to listen up and become the Kings you're destined to be.

60

*"I hope that you're the one
If not, you are the prototype
We'll tiptoe to the sun
And do thangs I know you like."*

Andre 3000

BLAME IT ON THE MUSIC

Artist: Andre 3000

Album: The Love Below (2003)

Prototype

When I was younger, I thought that every female I dated would be the woman that I was going to marry. Like most young people I was very naïve, I didn't understand phases and growth. My perception of love and life in general was limited to the relationships I witnessed growing up. The inconsistency and chaos made me want to hold on tight to anything that seemed good to me. I had felt the pain of losing things and people that I loved from an early age and it hindered me later on in life. I can say that I'm healed from my past trauma and I have my eyes on the future. I wonder what type of woman is the perfect fit for me. I notice so many things in women that attracts me to them. I admire women who have a welcoming spirit, it takes so much effort to remain that way in this ever changing world. Sometimes I'm ashamed about how much I lust after women, I can't help but to admire a lady with a nice physique. I understand that sexuality plays a role in attraction but I long for deeper connections. This song was introduced to me while I was watching an interview of artist Janelle Monae, I feel that this was not a coincidence. This woman personifies what a lady should be. She is creative, ambitious, humble, a visionary and truly a beautiful person amongst so many other things. She is a woman I admire a lot, her music is what this world needs, and her vision as an artist and goddess goes unmatched. She is a woman who demands attention by remaining true to who she is and she doesn't exploit her sexuality for money, which makes her even more desirable. Her intense approach to her life's work makes her perfect in my eyes. She represents the type of woman that I would want to have a union with and if she's not the one, then she's most definitely the PROTOTYPE.

BLAME IT ON THE MUSIC

61

*"Leaving all my fears to burn down
Push them all away so I can move on
Closer to my dreams
Feel it all over my being
Close your eyes and see what you believe."*

Goapele

BLAME IT ON THE MUSIC

Artist: Goapele

Album: Even Closer (2002)

Closer

Everything about this song is perfect, the melody is smooth and the words fit the beat so well. We all have goals in life and visions of how we want to live, this song is for the dreamers. Some people set their sights on what they want and they acquire it immediately. On the contrary, quite often the things that we hope and pray for seem impossible to grasp. We all possess our own unique ability to fantasize about anything we choose, we can use our imaginations to draw nearer to our dreams. Then again, our fantasies can remind us of how far-fetched our dreams really are. In this very moment an overwhelming sense of joy has come upon me. As I have mentioned before, my life hasn't always been the greatest. I was forced to make adult decisions at a young age, I've seen things no human should be exposed to as well. I've questioned God's existence, as well as my own, plenty of times. I wouldn't change anything that I've experienced in my life, aside from a few tragic deaths of my loved ones. I know my life is a testimony of so many things. I humbly accept every blessing I will receive, while I was busy trying to make a living I have manifested one of my dreams. At the beginning of 2013 I read a book called The Secret, by Rhonda Byrne. Reading this book has set me on a path of enlightenment and self-fulfillment, I set goals after reading this wonderful book. I neglected to look back at my goals, now I realize I have accomplished most of them. I became a basketball coach at my former high school, which has been a long time dream of mine. I started an online blog to share my thoughts that I often kept suppressed inside of me. I've started to work out regularly as well as adopt better eating habits. I had a vacation to Miami to try-out for a semi-pro basketball team. All these feats may seem small to you but the mean everything to me. There's a saying that I often hear successful people use which is, "act like you've been here before". To me it means to remain the same when you accomplish great things, I would normally heed to these words but at this moment I can't. I've achieved a major goal of mine which was to provide something to the world by publishing my own book. I didn't realize writing this would be a life changing venture for me, sort of like therapy sessions. I'm going to allow myself the opportunity to bask in the completion of my work. Of course I want to sell millions of copies, but I will not let numbers determine how I feel, the joy and happiness that I gained in the making of this book is success in my eyes. I hope I'm an example of what hard work and diligence can get you; if I can do it, so can you. This book is my gift to the world, I hope these words and the music can help you out as much as it has helped me.

BLAME IT ON THE MUSIC

Part 2 Preview: R&B

The entire experience of writing this book has truly been an amazing journey for me. These songs along with the artist who created them are such an inspiration to the world. When I listen to these songs they all mean something special to me. The songs remind me of my past good and bad times, they remind me how far I've come in life. There were periods when I felt like my life was a waste, I wanted to give up so many times. God used these individuals and their creative genius to lead me out of my horrible circumstances. I am proud to introduce these songs to people who may have never heard them. I am in no way speaking for the artists, I'm merely sharing my perspective on things they spoke about. I had so much fun writing this book that I've actually started on a possible sequel; the difference is that I will use all R&B songs to analyze and share how they've also inspired me. I felt like I should share some of those songs as a preview, so keep reading and I hope you enjoy!

BLAME IT ON THE MUSIC

Artist: Jaheim featuring Next

Album: Ghetto Love (2000)

Anything

This song brings back so many memories for me. My first car was a 1984 Buick Regal, I used to put this cd in and ride around blasting this track. This song is about love and being a provider for your significant other. One thing that I've noticed about relationships is people often put their partner's needs before their own. I do think that all successful relationships require self-lessness from both parties; this doesn't mean that a person should allow their mate to walk over them. I was introduced to the law of attraction by a friend of mine and the law states that we can have anything we ask for, no matter how big or small it is. It took me until I was into my early twenties to recognize that I could never fully appeal to anyone more than I could please myself. I spent most of my life catering to the needs of my family and friends. During those times I often disregarded the things that I wanted for the sake of providing for everyone else. The approach I was taking was very ineffective because I needed to focus on myself first. I was so angry when each of my relationships failed, without realizing the error in my ways. I actually expected failure without being conscious of my thoughts. I listened to people tell me what I was capable of, neglecting the feelings of greatness that I possessed. Like I said previously, the law of attraction gives us anything we ask for; our thoughts and the things we focus on the most are going to manifest in our lives. It doesn't matter whether those things are good or bad, whatever we give our energy and emotions to will be brought into existence. When my life was at its worst I allowed my thoughts to center around negativity. Now I'm aware that I have the power to create the experiences that I want, so I direct all of my efforts and energy on the things I want to have. When we finally recognize how easy life is this world will operate the way that the Universal God intended it to.

BLAME IT ON THE MUSIC

Artist: Destiny's Child

Album: Destiny Fulfilled (2004)

Cater To You

When I hear R&B songs about love and relationships they often have a negative vibe. There are so many songs out where the men are bashing women and vice versa. I understand that creativity can come out of negative experiences. When we start growing we must focus on what we want to experience and reject every thought of things that aren't beneficial to us. Cater To You is one of my all-time favorite songs because of its message. As a man I've been taught to be tough, tense and on edge all the time. Men end up neglecting their bodies and minds for the sake of being a provider for everyone around us. This song is every guy's dream, which is to be catered to by their companion. Since men don't regularly take the time to cater to our own needs, Destiny's Child offers to do it for us. This song gives other women so much insight on how they can help their man become relaxed and stress free. When I was younger I loved this song and I would secretly listen to it because I didn't want anyone to think that I was "soft". That's another problem we face as men, the perception of appearing weak. I asked a woman her thoughts on men liking this song and she said it was perfectly fine. I've learned to not really feel burdened by the way others view me, the song was made for men anyways. I've grown to understand that I can take the time out to relax and meet my own needs. What I love about grown women is the fact that they take the initiative to present feminine energy to their mates. It takes a woman's nurturing touch to help tame the beast in most men. My

BLAME IT ON THE MUSIC

advice to all women is to listen to this song and let the beautiful singers guide you through.

BLAME IT ON THE MUSIC

Artist: Anita Baker

Album: Giving You The Best That I Got (1988)

I Love You Just Because

Anita Baker is a remarkable singer with a plethora of hit songs. This song is probably my favorite one by her, it's a feel good tune. The reason why I love it so much is because of the relevance and simplicity of the lyrics. She speaks of her reason for loving her mate. I haven't been in many relationships but one thing I have always heard about women asking men is, "why do you love/like me". I've got this question a few times in my lifetime; those few times, I didn't have an answer either. I'll admit that I was shy, stubborn and completely clueless back then. I felt like I shouldn't have to present a paragraph about why I liked someone. I didn't understand how much people, women especially, need positive reinforcement. I look back now and laugh because I'm more aware. I've never been the guy that runs game and recites lines to women, I always said what I felt and kept things simple. If I say I love you, I mean it and I do my best to prove it with my actions. Simply saying I love you just because isn't viewed as acceptable, because you have to have at least one reason. I feel like the ego is what makes people want to hear the good things their mate views in them. Love is an everyday action and not just a few words. It's also perfectly fine to love someone just because of the person that they are.

BLAME IT ON THE MUSIC

Artist: The Temptations

Album: None

Beauty Is Only Skin Deep

I wonder what blind people use to judge other people. Do they just listen to people talk and assess their character, or do they have unique characteristics that people who can see don't possess? When I see a woman I use different words to describe how I feel about their looks. Anytime I hear the word sexy used to describe a woman I automatically assume that she has a nice body but she isn't the best looking in the face. Using the word pretty means that the woman has a nice looking face and she may or may not have the body to compliment her looks. Of course we all have different preferences of what we like. We all have a list that we hold up when we're on the dating trail. I personally prefer a woman who's educated, ambitious and well mannered. The things that we first notice are usually visual, so that's where we start judging. Sometimes we get caught up in looks so much that character and personality doesn't matter. It's tough to see past the images that people portray, especially in the beginning. The word beautiful to me represents something rare, unique and breathtaking. This is my all-time favorite track by The Temptations. It speaks of not getting so caught up in the facade of a nice body and pretty face. The important factors are seeking love and natural interactions. When I say that a woman is beautiful I am judging her from the inside first. The substance of a woman's heart is what determines whether she has beauty in my opinion, it has little to do with her looks. Society has been the biggest influence on what beauty looks like and I think they often get it wrong. I rarely see black women, especially darker skinned women,

BLAME IT ON THE MUSIC

get the beautiful description. I'm here to tell every woman that if you seek to truly be a beautiful person, all you have to do is develop the depth of your heart first.

BLAME IT ON THE MUSIC

Artist: Al Green

Album: Still In Love With You (1972)

Love And Happiness

The way that I've been raised has led me to believe that these two things are what's important in life. Love and happiness are things that each and every one of us is seeking. I didn't see enough examples of what it really was, most of the people settled and lived just to get by. These two things can mean something different to each and every individual. Love is the language of the Universal God, all creations were made from love and with love in mind. I think that the word love has been altered to fit people's needs in particular moments, instead of having a concrete description. I often get confused listening to people talk about love and being in love. When it's explained in relationships it always seems forced to me. I feel like true love doesn't have to mean you're sacrificing, I prefer to say it's compromising. When there's sacrifice in a relationship someone is usually taking a loss. Compromise is more geared towards finding a medium, where two people are collaborating to benefit each other. I want a love that is natural, passionate and fulfilling. I am willing to work diligently towards those things. I refuse to be with someone who doesn't motivate and inspire me to be a better man, not only for her but for myself as well. There's a time in everyone's life where we should evaluate the people we spend significant time pursuing. I feel like this applies to our family members as well, we should all want better for one another. Once we place value on displaying genuine love to everyone, happiness will be a residual effect of that. We have to start by loving ourselves, by doing that we allow others the exact same luxury.

www.ingramcontent.com/pod-product-compliance
Lightning Source LLC
Chambersburg PA
CBHW071459040426
42444CB00008B/1415